The Cryonics Estate Planning Handbook:
Maybe You CAN Take It With You!

Rudi Hoffman & Peggy Hoyt

© 2020 Rudi Hoffman and Peggy Hoyt, all rights reserved.

No part of this book may be reproduced, stored in a retrieval system or transmitted by any means without the sole consent and written permission of the authors.

First published in January 2021
Formatted by Sean Donovan www.SeanDon.com

ISBN: 9798590531486
Imprint: Independently published

Printed in the United States of America

Contents

1. The Journey Begins 1
2. Can You REALLY "Take It With You?" Why Thoughtful Estate Planning Is Crucial for Cryonicists 17
3. Time Out! How Am I Going to Pay for This? How Life Insurance Provides Smart Leverage 35
4. Beginning the Cryonics Estate Planning Process 51
5. Does a Traditional Last Will and Testament Work for Cryonicists? 59
6. Your Cryonics Friendly Living Trust With Your Personal Revival Trust™ (Oh, and Your Pour-Over Will)............67
7. Time Out Again! What's the Deal With Trustees and Trust Protectors?..81
8. Cryonicists Need to Avoid Forced Guardianship. Let's Talk About How to Do That!..91
9. Your Cryonics Friendly Durable Financial Power of Attorney 107
10. Healthcare Directives and Your Cryonics Friendly Durable Healthcare Power of Attorney 125
11. What About the Health Information Portability and Accountability Act and Your Cryonics Plans?............133
12. Your Cryonics Friendly Living Will 139
13. Avoiding Autopsy Is Imperative for Cryonicists! 145

14. Additional Considerations for Your Cryonics Estate Plan 153
15. Moving Toward Immortality: Four Simple Action Steps 167

Appendices 176
Contacts and References 192
Glossary of Terms 200
About the Authors 205

"Begin with the end in mind."
Stephen Covey, *The Seven Habits of Highly Effective People*

"We cannot insure success, but we can deserve it."
John Adams, in biography *John Adams* by David McCullough

Chapter One
The Journey Begins

Introduction

Okay. We get it! Until this moment, planning, estate planning, and particularly Cryonics Estate Planning have not been on your list as fun, easy, or possibly even doable endeavors. But together, Dear Reader, we are going on a journey to change that perception.

Mission Statement

The mission of this book is to make Cryonics Estate Planning as clear, straightforward, and fun as possible. Here are the four major concepts we intend for you to take away from your reading:

Four Takeaways

1. Cryonics is a legitimate, though currently unproven, medical intervention. Assuming Cryonics does indeed work and you are revived, it will probably be in a really spectacular and intriguing future.
2. Cryonicists will want to have resources to fund their resuscitation and to provide options for their future life through careful Cryonics Estate Planning.

3. Cryonics and Cryonics Estate Planning may well be affordable for you through the leverage of life insurance and specifically designed annuities.

4. There are resources and people to help you in your research and decision- making. Peggy and Rudi are two of those helpful and accessible resources!

Just What IS Cryonics?

Rudi writing: A quick review to make sure we are clear on a few basics. Cryonics is the medical process of using the best available technology to preserve biological structure to possibly enable resuscitation of humans at a future point. As this is written in late 2020, the current "state of the art" in cryopreservation involves a process called "vitrification." Briefly, this is perfusion with a biological "antifreeze" which virtually eliminates the freezing of the water that makes up the major part of our physiology. This enables biological structures to be preserved with a high degree of fidelity, even at a fine-grained cellular level.

At this point in history, Cryonics is considered a legitimate, though experimental and unproven, technology for life extension. Like any other advanced medical intervention, there are no guarantees of success provided by Cryonics or Cryonics vendors.

Because of rigorous ongoing scientific effort, however, the field of Cryonics is an increasingly accepted possibility in life extension options.

Cryonics has been around conceptually since 1964 with the publishing of Robert Ettinger's seminal book *The Prospect of Immortality* and the incorporation of the Alcor Life Extension Foundation as a non-profit organization in 1972. However, Cryonics as a medical intervention has taken fifty years to become a more mainstream medical consideration, and it can be fairly stated that many would consider the field aspirational science. The confluence of exponentially advancing research in nano-technology, synthetic biology, health extension, and senescence attenuation and reversal, all provide credibility to reversible cryopreservation. And, while Cryonics is continuing to gain scientific validity, current protocols do not enable fully reversible cryopreservation of even mice, much less humans.

The obvious premise of Cryonics is to send us forward in time when technology can revive us. And this resuscitation will not just bring us back as the damaged, wizened, decrepit, senescent entity that was cryopreserved. The purpose of Cryonics is to resuscitate us as vibrant, youthful entities who feel as good as we did on the best day of our lives. Any technology that can bring us back, fix the difficulties that occurred prior to our being declared legally dead, and repair any damage that may have resulted from the Cryonics process itself will arguably also be able to cure the ravages of aging.

So the idea here, to be clear, is not just to be "revived" from our Cryonics nap in the future, but is instead to wake up feeling levels of joy, energy, and enthusiasm that many of us only had at some vaguely remembered day in our younger years. This strong statement is confirmed by current age-reversal research occurring across the globe.

And What Is Cryonics Estate Planning?

The concept of Cryonics Estate Planning is to have all of the above *AND* the additional benefit of having an abundance of resources!

Just imagine, for a moment, how remarkably wonderful life could be under these circumstances. Your zest for living has been fine tuned, your body and neurochemistry adjusted for optimal performance; you have the wisdom and experience of many years. AND you don't have worries about such mundane matters as having enough assets to cover your needs and wants!

As I write this, I can feel my inner skeptic being wary of the "selling" of some wonderful state of future utopia. Maybe your skepticism/cynicism filter functions like mine does. Your inner Captain Kirk orders, "Shields up!" to protect you from this manipulation.

You can relax, Dear Reader, and your inner James Kirk can order "Shields down," because we are not going to promise you bliss in an afterlife to manipulate you into doing Cryonics and establishing a Cryonics Estate Plan.

This is a scientific and technological endeavor, not a faith based undertaking that requires us to leave our rational and modern epistemology behind.

If you are reading this book, you are probably aware of this and other concerns about the idea of Cryonics, and have perhaps made up your mind based on your ongoing research and personal risk/reward matrix.

Part of the mission in this book is to give you a glimpse into the future, and we are not talking about a future that is "out there." We are talking about your personal future, what your future days could be like if you had a trust fund with hundreds of millions of dollars or the equivalent of that amount. Of course, having financial resources won't solve all problems, or even all of our personal problems. But it would provide a different set of problems that most of us would rather deal with.

Yes, it is okay for you and me to take a moment to dream about a personal future which could be unbelievably great. You are reading and taking action on the ideas in this book to make that future a reality. Let's get started on making that happen!

Who Are You? Where Are You in This Process?
Is this book for you? Let's ask some questions to find out.

1. Are you curious about the future?
2. Have you been researching the possibilities of cryopreservation?
3. Maybe you are already signed up for cryopreservation?
4. Have you wondered, "Hey, if Cryonics works and I am revived in the future, how will I make a living? My skills, contacts, education...all would likely be obsolete. Wouldn't it be great if I had a large asset base to provide some options?"
5. Have you been told by a well meaning (but uninformed) friend, estate planner, or attorney that... "It is not possible to execute any directives that would function as Cryonics planning directives.". . ?
6. If Cryonics works, would you be interested in a chance to wake up really, really rich?

If you answered "Yes" to any of the above, you have come to the right place!

This book is written for anyone investigating Cryonics and Cryonics Estate Planning. If you are new to Cryonics and curious about the Cryonics Estate Planning process, if you are a seasoned cryonicist who has been signed up for decades, or if you are an estate planning attorney interested in exploring ideas related to Cryonics Estate Planning, you should find this book helpful. It is a practical guidebook that will be fun and easy to read and understand, whether you have any background in these subjects or not. (Okay, fun may be pushing it a bit.)

You, Dear Reader, are part of the process in creating an evidenced-based, dynamic, legitimate field we will call "Cryonics Estate Planning." Let's begin this journey with a skeptical but open mind and a seriousness of purpose proportional to the enormous potential for the benefit you may realize from taking action on these words and ideas.

If Cryonics and Cryonics Estate Planning can be made to work, the possibilities and upsides are almost certainly beyond our wild imaginings of how amazing being alive could be. Is there a future You who could be swimming the oceans testing out your new upgraded water breathing gills? And maybe one who loves the freedom of zero gravity acrobatics in space? Perhaps a future You who enables non-human animals to have direct mind-to-mind contact with humans? Or a future You who figures out how to create a range of positive cognitive states for your fellow earthlings in order to reduce the suffering of all sentient beings? **Do you think it is reasonable to assume you could do more for yourself and** *others if you had a large amount of money to spread around in that future?*

Who Are We? Why Are We Qualified to Write This Book?

Rudi here: My co-author Peggy Hoyt and I are probably...almost certainly...the foremost experts in the world in the growing and very specialized fields of Cryonics Funding and Cryonics Estate Planning.

Let me give you a quick summary of our credentials.

- I am the world's leading writer of life insurance for the purpose of funding cryopreservation. About 60% of the humans signed up for Cryonics on Planet Earth who are adequately and properly funded have accomplished this with the help of Hoffman Financial Engineering. This percentage is derived by dividing the number of global cryonicists by the number of Cryonics clients placed with Hoffman Financial Engineering.
- I have been licensed and active in the life insurance and investments business since 1978, which is forty-two years as of this writing.
- I hold the three highest and most prestigious designations in financial planning, Certified Financial Planner®, Chartered Life Underwriter®, and

Chartered Financial Consultant®. I am licensed and authorized in 49 states and the District of Columbia.

Our firm has helped folks fund both Cryonics and Cryonics Estate Planning, as well as fund more traditional insurance, investment, and financial planning. Since 1994, when I personally signed up for cryonic suspension, I have helped literally thousands of intelligent humans make informed decisions about Cryonics.

Peggy has been practicing law for more than 25 years. In addition to her MBA in Finance, she holds certification as a Board-Certified Specialist from the Florida Bar in Wills, Trusts and Estates and in Elder Law. Prior to becoming a lawyer, she worked as a financial advisor for a major brokerage house. She is passionate about helping people achieve their estate planning goals and has focused her practice on unique niche specialties, including planning for persons with special needs, planning for pets, and of course, planning for Cryonicists.

In short, Cryonics Funding and Cryonics Estate Planning are a central part of our professions. We are good at this stuff!

But we are also deeply aware that both Cryonics and Cryonics Estate Planning are emerging fields with areas of uncertainty that are "baked in" to the nature of these endeavors.

It is not our intention to pretend that we have all the answers. The field is too new for ANY professionals to make that claim. It IS our intention to frame the questions in a meaningful and informed way. And we will share what some other very intelligent, highly educated, and in some cases extremely wealthy people are doing regarding Cryonics Estate Planning. These are people like you, who have taken action to put Cryonics arrangements AND Cryonics Estate Planning arrangements in place.

Just as in virtually every field of endeavor, in Cryonics and Cryonics Estate Planning there are "known problems" and "possible" and "optimal" solutions to these problems. As physicist/philosopher David Deutch observes in his book *The Beginning of Infinity*, the real paradigm shift in the Enlightenment was not merely the questioning of religious authority. It was the foundational epistemological shift in which ALL ideas are expected to be questioned. In this "meritocracy of ideas," the best ideas emerge and evolve through rigorous and reasoned thought. **As the authors of the first book on this particular topic, we hope to encourage rigorous dialogue and advance a practical framework for Cryonics Estate Planning.**

About the Book Format
This book is a collaborative project, with Attorney Peggy Hoyt and Certified Financial Planner Rudi Hoffman writing jointly. From time to time, we write individually, and we will identify

these sections. Sometimes we will talk directly to each of you, Dear Readers, identified cleverly by the notation, "Dear Reader."

We will reintroduce you to a fictional couple you may remember from Rudi's first book on Cryonics funding. We'll mix some stories of real people into the content about Cryonics Estate Planning, people and situations you can relate to. And we will explain the WHY of Cryonics Estate Planning.

So let's reintroduce Jerry and Pat.

Rudi again: You might have (and may I respectfully say I *hope* you have!) read *The Affordable Immortal: Maybe You CAN Beat Death and Taxes!* by Rudi Hoffman, published in 2018 and available on Amazon. This was the book that took me a mere 17 years to complete and introduced fictional characters named Jerry and Pat Reynolds. While fictional, Jerry and Pat represent a composite of multiple real human beings who have signed up for Cryonics and are considering or have completed Cryonics Estate Plans.

Our fictional friends Pat and Jerry live in California where she is a hospital administrator and he is a software developer. They have two sons, now 14 and 16, and two new adopted rescue dogs. After copious research and soul searching, the couple met (virtually) with Rudi over a year ago. Rudi helped them contract with Alcor for their cryopreservation and fund the process through life insurance. Alcor Life Extension Foundation is one of the primary Cryonics organizations in the United States, along with The Cryonic Institute in Michigan and the California based American Cryonics Society.

Jerry and Pat's concerns about costs, logistics, reputation risk, and keeping their friends and extended family happy with their Cryonics decision are a very real part of nearly every Cryonics signup story. And in this book, their process of creating a Cryonics Estate Plan should be informative to you, Dear Reader, as you contemplate your options for the future.

A Personal Story

Rudi still writing. When I was researching signing up for Cryonics in 1994, I had a lot of questions. Many of these had to do with the technology and medical pieces of the Cryonics puzzle. And the concerns about the logistics involved. And the integrity of the people involved. And the structure and financial integrity of the organization. And, and, and… It took me about six months of research, in which I did a lot of reading, spent a lot of hours on the websites of various Cryonics organizations, and . . . something else. I am almost embarrassed to divulge this, but it is the truth.

I took up WAY too much time on phone calls to the membership director of Alcor. Because, frankly, I was lazy, and preferred to get my questions answered via phone calls instead of reading the websites, plowing through massive amounts of opinions, facts, and research. The search engines in 1994 were not nearly as effective as ours now and I wanted a personal relationship with an "expert" who understood I was a smart guy asking smart questions.

Here is the point to this story. The most compelling component of all of this research and time was that there remained many UNANSWERED questions!

This was and remains the distinction between a genuine scientific endeavor and a cult of true believers who feel they already *have* all the answers. Perhaps you, like me, really believe you try to make your decisions on the best information you can get. And, given the demographics of the people who are interested in cryopreservation, there is a pretty good chance that the brain reading these words has a tendency toward rationalism and skepticism. Maybe you are skeptical of the claims of religions; maybe you are skeptical of the claims of politics. Maybe you are especially skeptical when an "authority figure" expects you to believe them without good reasons and good explanations.

Unfounded certainty - - in any area where there CANNOT be certainty - - is a red flag to me. And I suspect it is to you as well. If I had been told by the membership director of Alcor, "Oh, Mr. Hoffman, don't worry about how the Cryonics technicians are going to arrive exactly when you need them, just moments before there is a legal pronouncement of death. We have all of that figured out!" you would not be reading these words, because I would have realized that no one could possibly "have that all figured out!"

My BS detector would have gone into the red zone, and I bet yours would have as well. Instead, my questions were often met with a simple, "Well, we don't know for sure, but here is what the research is pointing to."

In responding to my many questions about the logistics of how cryopreservation could work, given that I live thousands of kilometers from Alcor, there was a frank acknowledgement that logistics are a known problem in Cryonics. And, in the spirit of good engineering, good science, and good philosophy, there was an attitude of "Problems are inevitable. And, problems are solvable."

For instance, my many concerns about logistics and how Cryonics could work for me were met with a reality-based discussion of exactly what the components of the problem were, and what specific behaviors I could take to increase my odds of a good cryopreservation.

This is the level of integrity and credibility that we as the authors will be bringing you regarding the next steps for serious cryonicists. This is what you deserve as a highly intelligent, skeptical, sophisticated human investing their time and money in this book.

This book is written to the You who could…and may…exist in a future of gradations of joy. We hope you'll share the feedback and questions that arise as you read and explore this topic with us. Here's to our future!

Meanwhile, let's tune in on Jerry and Pat as they discuss *their* preferred future and consider what it might mean for them to take the next steps toward developing an estate plan that would promote their Cryonics objectives.

Chapter Two
Can You REALLY "Take It With You?" Why Thoughtful Estate Planning Is Crucial for Cryonicists

Since signing up as cryonicists, Pat and Jerry have been feeling quite satisfied with their decisions. After last month's passing of their close friend Anton, however, and observing how Anton's family was already fighting viciously over Anton's estate, they have been discussing what additional preparation could reduce the risk of that chaos for *their* family.

Good Estate Planning Is Vital to Preserve Good Relationships

Like many Americans, Pat and Jerry have a basic will and some generic healthcare directives, but after only minimal research they have realized that those documents are insufficient. The more they find out, the more they feel their children, pets, and estate are not well protected; nor have they taken advantage of any special planning they might do to gear up for the future they hope to have together with loved ones.

Let's join them as they are enjoying dinner in their modest California bungalow. Pat stopped between bites. "It's kind of nice, isn't it, Jerry, that the boys are both at a friend's tonight? I've been wanting to talk to you because I've been thinking a lot about Anton's death and what an incredible mess he left everyone in. What really disturbs me is we know how smart he was and how much he loved his family.

"And now," she continued, "we are having to see the absolute disaster that has occurred since he died. Did you know that his two daughters are no longer talking to each other or to their Mother? And I think there may be some lawsuits filed against their own family members! It makes me wonder, how could anyone as smart as Anton be so clueless about providing clear directions about his assets?"

Jerry looked up sadly as he scooped a generous portion of salad on his plate. Pat knew how close he had been to Anton. "It is so sad, Pat! Can you imagine how different life at Anton's house would be right now if he had taken the time to put a good estate plan together?"

"Yah," Pat answered. "His kids would be acting like the adults they are and not treating each other like arch enemies! But in their defense, Anton left them with lots of tough decisions to make."

"True," Jerry concurred, "and to be fair, Anton isn't the only example. I was reading an article, I think it was in Forbes, that said less than one third of Americans have even basic estate planning documents like a will and advance medical directives. And you always hear about celebrities and rich guys who manage to slop up their estate plans. Is the Michael Jackson estate *still* in litigation?

"Pat, the biggest lesson is to be sure we have taken care of each other and we really need to have much better provisions in place for our kids' security. And I don't think we should be too harsh in judging Anton, because we haven't gotten around to doing *our* estate planning either."

Passing the vegetables, Pat nodded. "Guilty as charged and our boys could suffer because of it! And Jerry, I'm also worried about the dogs. I don't want them to end up back in a shelter like the one we rescued them from. They might get separated and might not have happy lives the way they do now."

Jerry fed a green bean to their dachshund/poodle mix Daisy while he responded. "We have our Cryonics arrangements settled and funded and I'm really pleased about that. But seeing the negative example of Anton has me motivated to actually DO what we have put off for years. We HAVE to set things up right for our kids, our pets, our money - and frankly, for our future selves!"

Pat nodded. "It really is time! I know why I have put it off over the years . . .it just seems so overwhelming! How about for a first action step if we just try to learn more about how the Cryonics thing fits into an estate plan? Maybe talk to Rudi Hoffman to get some direction? He did a great job hooking us up with our Cryonics funding, and he seems to know a lot about this stuff."

"A very cool idea! Sorry I didn't think of it first! He DID say to call him with questions anytime. How about if I make an appointment with him online?" Jerry looked over at the refrigerator. "Aha! His magnet card is still on the fridge! And I'll put his number in our phones, so we'll have it whenever we need it."

"Hmm! Sounds like a good step forward! Uh, and Jerry dear? Didn't we agree that we would not feed the dogs at the table?"

Jerry smiled and fed another green bean to Daisy. "Blame the boys; they started it!"

So, Is Cryonics Estate Planning a Real Thing?

Jerry set an appointment to talk with Rudi on Rudi's website RudiHoffman.com. At the specified time, he dialed Rudi at 386-235-7834 and he and Pat joined Rudi on a Zoom call. Jerry hid his grin when he saw Rudi in his slightly disheveled office, wearing his signature bright colored golf shirt and shorts, not looking at all like a conservatively dressed financial type.

"Jerry! Great to hear from you. And hello, Pat. How have you been? It has been a while since we talked last. What's happening with you folks these days?"

"Things are great here. We are really happy with our Cryonics funding life insurance policies, and of course we have completed the Alcor paperwork as well, so all is solid and fine on that front. And that variable annuity with the income guarantee you made available has been doing remarkably well! But, Rudi, Pat and I have been talking and some questions came up, and we thought we would check with you about them."

"Sounds good; what's on your mind?"

"Well, we've been thinking about the future and of course we want to make sure our boys are looked after, and at a recent virtual Cryonics conference I went to, I heard there may be ways to take your assets with you during cryopreservation.

"And we recently adopted two rescue dogs and we got to thinking about how we could make sure they were taken care of too! Do you know if any of this is even a real possibility?"

The question clearly pleased Rudi, who chuckled and said with a big smile, "Oh, wow. What remarkably good timing! I have just completed a book on this very topic with my co-author and attorney Peggy Hoyt. The short answer is: Yes, it is indeed possible to establish a Cryonics Estate Plan designed to deal with these exact issues. A lot of very educated and intelligent cryonicists have been working on the questions of how we can take assets with us while we are cryopreserved. In fact, I have been working on this personally for over 26 years. Stand by; let me show you something."

Rudi went off-screen for a moment and came back holding a 3-inch burgundy binder. He held the spine of this thick document up to the camera as he spoke. "This is a copy of my own Cryonics Estate Plan, including my 'Personal Revival Trust™,' which is the brilliant proprietary format Peggy Hoyt's firm has developed *specifically* for their cryonicist clients. About ten years ago, Peggy set this up for me and did one for my wife Dawn. In addition to being a Personal Revival Trust™, it is also designed to establish protocols to make sure our pets are well taken care of if both of us are in the Cryonics dewar. And it has asset protection and tax planning provisions for my wife and me while we are alive *prior* to cryopreservation. The bottom line is that Cryonics Estate Planning IS a real thing, and I am excited that you are interested in learning about it.

"In fact, Jerry and Pat, since you are such loyal clients, I will send you a PDF of the book and also priority mail a copy of the physical book to you so we can refer to sections together."

Special Challenges and Opportunities of Cryonics Estate Planning

Rudi took a moment to make himself a note to send the book in two formats, and then looked back at the camera intently. "Clearly there are special challenges and opportunities in planning your estate when Cryonics is concerned!"

Pat leaned a bit further into camera range, definitely interested. "That's kind of what we thought, Rudi, but we simply don't know what we don't know about this arena."

"I understand completely, Pat. And there are a few things to think about which make Cryonics Estate Planning a bit of an interesting challenge. May I go into these things on a broad conceptual basis right now?"

"Absolutely, Rudi," responded Jerry. "That's why we called."

The Rule Against Perpetuities

"Well, friends, Cryonics Estate Planning has had to overcome a few issues, which is why it took me the last few decades of research and networking to get to the point where we could write this book about it. The information we'll go over here is literally the work of over 26 years. Initially, some of the people and even higher end attorneys I spoke with told me Cryonics planning could never work because of a thing called the 'Rule Against Perpetuities,' which basically says a trust cannot last indefinitely. The good news? It turns out that this is not applicable to all states, and that something like seventeen states have either abolished or extended the rule. Florida, for instance, where my trust is based, enables a trust to go from the time of death for 360 years! Other states have basically unlimited trust periods, and since we can set the legal home of the trust in one of these states, the ==‘Rule Against Perpetuities’== is not much of a problem. When you get your copy of the *Handbook*, check out **Appendix F** for state specific comparisons."

How We Can Overcome the "Dead Don't Have Rights" Question

Rudi saw that Pat and Jerry were intrigued, so he continued. "What is a more genuine concern about Cryonics Estate Planning is that once you are *legally* pronounced as 'dead' (which has to happen for your life insurance policies to pay off and for the cryogenic cooling to be initiated), you have NO legal rights! You are no longer a person in the eyes of the law. Like the dead parrot in that old Monty Python sketch is an 'ex-parrot,' you are an 'ex-person!'

"Because of the research you folks and most cryonicists have done, you almost certainly understand that 'death' is not really a binary yes/no proposition. But the law is not yet ready for that kind of fine-grained question. As far as the law is concerned, if a medical professional pronounces you 'dead,' you are a non-entity with no rights."

"Yes, last night in bed I was thinking about that exact question," chimed in Jerry. "While I understand that death may have a much more elastic non-binary description than most people realize, the reality is that many people describe the humans who are cryopreserved as corpses. I gotta say it kind of does make sense to me that corpses don't have rights or personhood."

"Good point, Jerry," observed Rudi. "And you are right about the general idea here. Cryonics organizations, of course, refer to their cryopreserved members as 'patients,' not corpses. These are simply patients who are waiting for the appropriate technology to be restored to full personhood.

"But in designing feasible Cryonics trusts, our mission is NOT to create new laws, or push the boundaries to redefine Cryonics patients as fully human. Pragmatically, we want to work within established legal structures. Success in this field is structuring things in such a way that your planning does NOT end up being adjudicated as a landmark court case."

The Concept of the Dynasty Trust

Rudi continued. "We are essentially using a 'Dynasty Trust' structure that does not require new laws to be created before it can effectively function for Cryonics patients. The Dynasty Trust has been around for centuries. It has historically been used by wealthy people who want to provide for future generations, while maintaining control over the distribution of their assets, even after death. For example, Jerry, let's pretend for a moment that you are really wealthy, and your granddaddy went to Harvard, and your daddy went to Harvard, and you did too. You want your kids and grandkids and great grandkids to have the same opportunity to attend Harvard. To accomplish this goal, you can establish a Dynasty Trust that directs the trustee to pay for college tuition, provided the beneficiary attends Harvard. That is called 'control from the grave.' But we want to do something slightly different. We want to have 'control from the Cryonics dewar!'"

"Ah...I think I get it!" exclaimed Jerry. "Instead of trying to create new laws or have a court case to define personhood for Cryonics patients, this format addresses that whole question with law that is *already* established! And these Dynasty Trusts have been proven to work?"

"The general answer to that question is absolutely yes," responded Rudi. "However, while we are obviously too early in the curve to have proof that any Cryonics trust works, we have very good reasons to believe that this venerable, time-tested estate planning structure will do exactly what it is designed to do and has done so successfully for decades.

"So, yes, we are making a bit of history in setting these trusts up. But, just imagine if you two had the foresight and vision to set up such a trust. And that you now are not only alive in an amazing future, but you have dramatically enhanced resources! In short, if we are smart enough and lucky enough, there is a realistic chance that we could wake up truly wealthy!"

"Wow. . . that does sound pretty good," said Pat slowly, obviously considering the ramifications of this remarkable information. "But there are certainly a lot of things for us to think about regarding how to put together our estate plan, as well as the Cryonics and pet planning piece.

"I am beginning to understand that Cryonics Estate Planning is indeed a legitimate field, and that you and your colleagues have been working at this for a long time. I already have a bunch of questions about this, like who would manage the money while Jerry and I are taking our 'dewar nap'? How long might it take to revive us? And if it takes a long time, how can we be sure our trustees will be able to stay around? And, if they were getting a percentage to manage our assets, what would be their incentive to revive us? And we know countries and currencies change over time; how can we expect to even know what will be a prudent store of value over extended time? I'm sorry, Rudi, but I must say that I am interested, even fascinated, by this idea, but we certainly will want to get at least some of these questions answered."

Pat realized she had been talking a long time, and when she stopped, there was a long pause, with Jerry looking a bit awkward and Rudi looking thoughtful. Rudi let the silence hang for a few more beats.

"Bravo!" he then exclaimed enthusiastically. "Pat, I am delighted you brought up these genuinely relevant and important questions. You have hit upon some of the most central challenges of estate planning and especially Cryonics Estate Planning. The good news is that we can indeed answer most of these questions, as well as a bunch of other questions we will come up with jointly. The even better news is that we now have a paved path forward for some of these issues because of the visionary work which has already been done in the field."

"Well, I've got a question, too, before we go any farther," Jerry added. "Just what kind of components would go into a Cryonics Estate Plan?"

"Great question, Jerry. Let me pull up a document that shows the basics and I'll hit the magic screen-sharing button.

"Here's an overview of what might be included in your Cryonics Estate Plan. The GOOD NEWS? You two have already taken care of the first big step! You've both already signed up for Cryonics and have solidly funded your arrangements.

"So, after you create a summary of your assets, your Cryonics Estate Plan will typically include, at a minimum, the following legal instruments. The parentheses show the chapter that deals with this component in the *Handbook*."

Components of Your Cryonics Estate Plan

1. **FIRST AND ESSENTIAL: A Contract with a Cryopreservation Organization** (i.e. Alcor or Cryonics Institute or American Cryonics Society) where arrangements have been made **in advance** for the purpose of conducting the cryopreservation at the time of legal death. Note: this contract will likely require proof you have a dedicated life insurance policy and/or sufficient assets structured in a guaranteed annuity to pay for your cryopreservation (Chapter Three).

2. **A Cryonics Friendly Personal Revival Trust™ with Pour-Over Last Will and Testament** that allows cryonicists to personally control their assets while they are alive and healthy, plan for the management of their assets in the event of mental incapacity, and after their legal death, preserve assets for their future reanimation. The Pour-Over Will transfers any left-over assets (those assets not already titled into the Trust) from the probate estate into the Personal Revival Trust™ (Chapter Six).

3. **A Cryonics Friendly Pre-Need Guardian Declaration** to nominate in advance those persons the cryonicist would choose to determine their capacity, in the event

there is ever a guardianship proceeding (Chapter Eight).

4. **A Cryonics Friendly Durable Financial Power of Attorney** to nominate an agent to make financial and legal decisions in case of the mental incapacity of the cryonicist (Chapter Nine).

5. **A Cryonics Friendly Healthcare Directive** with specialized Cryonics provisions that includes the appointment of a healthcare surrogate for assistance in making everyday medical care decisions along with **Health Insurance Portability and Accountability Act** (HIPAA) documentation that allows your surrogate to access your medical information. Forms and requirements are state specific and use various names for these directives and processes. For example, the Durable Medical Power of Attorney position is variously referred to in different states as a Healthcare Proxy, Healthcare Agent, or Healthcare Surrogate (Chapters Ten and Eleven).

6. **A Cryonics Friendly Living Will** that addresses the unique concerns of the cryonicist as the end of this lifetime emerges (Chapter Twelve).

7. **An Objection to Autopsy** for the purpose of preventing an unauthorized autopsy which could delay or impede the possibility of a successful cryopreservation (Chapter Thirteen).

Why Estate Planning, Especially Cryonics Estate Planning, Is NOT a Do-It-Yourself Project

Pat looked up at the camera. "Wow! This is some SERIOUS stuff!! Rudi, Jerry – this does NOT sound like a DIY project!!" Rudi concurred. "Pat, I think you are absolutely correct! While in our *Handbook* we showed how Cryonics Estate Planning is accessible and understandable, this does not mean you should try to 'go it alone.'

"Cryonics Estate Planning is not a do-it-yourself project any more than the actual cryopreservation itself. The committed cryonicist will want to assemble the best possible team of individuals who have one common goal - the successful preservation, maintenance and revival of the cryonicist.

"We understand that you (and by the nature of this book, you, Dear Reader) are self-sufficient and highly capable in using the 'just in time' virtual education now available at your fingertips to DIY many projects."

Rudi continued. "*However*, Cryonics Estate Planning is such a new and developing field of the law, there IS no 'boilerplate' language to pick up from the Internet, or even from the skeletal trust documents available from your Cryonics organization. There IS no public library of model Cryonics Estate Plans. Each case will by its nature be unique and complex. This will NOT be the time to be 'penny wise and pound foolish!' You will want the BEST and most experienced minds available to ensure your BEST possible future!

"I recently had some specialty surgery, and for the operation I went to a doctor who specialized in exactly what I needed done, not a generalist with passing knowledge.

"Your Cryonics Estate Plan will need to take into account the most current scientific, technical, financial and legal developments available. You will need persons who can coordinate with various professionals as well as work with your cryopreservation organization.

"And you will need processes put in place to assure your plan stays up to date with changes in your life, changes in the law, and changes in the way you want to leave assets for your beneficiaries, including your future self. In short, you need a Cryonics Estate Plan that can provide the resources and professionals to maintain you as a respected cryonicists for decades, if not hundreds of years."

STOP! Can I Afford to Do This? Encouragement: You Can Almost Certainly Afford to Create A Solid Cryonics Estate Plan

Jerry put up both hands. "WHOA!! So, how would this work? And, Rudi, to be frank, we aren't wealthy people. You recall our basic financial picture from before. Can we afford this?"

Pat reiterated Jerry's concern. "Thanks for asking that, Jerry! I have the same issue!"

Rudi grinned. "You've asked one of my favorite questions, Pat and Jerry! Many of our best clients who do Cryonics and Cryonics Estate Planning ARE NOT WEALTHY. (And, to be fair, some are…and we like them as well!). Shall we talk about some funding possibilities?"

Chapter Three
Time Out! How Am I Going to Pay for This? How Life Insurance Provides Smart Leverage

Rudi began, "Pat, Jerry, (and you, Dear Reader): you are asking the logical 'Can I Afford This?' question. Let me emphasize a critical concept at the outset of our funding discussion."

MOST PEOPLE FUND CRYONICS AND THEIR CRYONICS ESTATE PLAN WITH LIFE INSURANCE
"Because of the amazing leverage created by life insurance, people from all walks of life *can* be signed up and properly funded for Cryonics. If you are a currently signed cryonicist, odds are excellent that you have funded the cost of your cryopreservation through life insurance.

"And, even more remarkably, people from all walks of life can have a solid Cryonics Estate Plan which is also funded with the 'magic' of life insurance technology.

"Most people creating Cryonics trusts also use the smart leverage of life insurance to create a large income tax-free pot of money to go into that Cryonics trust! Please hear me loud and clear on this point. You do NOT need to be wealthy to create and fund a Cryonics trust, since life insurance can be used to fund the trust."

Pat and Jerry's Cryonics Funding Example

"You recall, Jerry and Pat, after your extensive research, soul-searching, values clarification discussion, budget tweaking (and a lot of pages in our last book!), you finally applied and were each approved for a $400,000 Index Universal Life policy. You intentionally and rationally obtained a life insurance policy with a higher face amount than was currently required by your Cryonics organization. The purpose of that 'over-funding,' of course, was to handle the future cost increases you expect to occur due to inflation and likely technological improvements.

"You both agreed that the coverage beyond the amount required to fund your Cryonics would be available to the survivor to help raise your children and to replace the income you each represent to your family. And, because the policies were well funded Index Universal Life policies, you were able to budget these programs not just as life insurance, but also as long-term tax-free savings vehicles."

The Power of Financial Leverage

The videoconference was now in full swing, and Rudi was in full didactic mode.

"Remember our previous discussions. I know some of what we will talk about here is review for you guys, but it sometimes helps to remind ourselves of the basics. Jerry, Pat, have you ever pulled out a nail with the claw of a hammer? It is really kind of fun. You position the hammer so the claw grabs the head of the nail, and you use the remarkable leverage of the hammer to pull out that pesky nail.

"The concept of leverage has been around for a long time. Archimedes is alleged to have said, 'Give me a lever long enough and a solid place to stand, and I can move the earth.' (I say alleged because it's hard to know exactly what anyone said several thousand years ago, so maybe we shouldn't pretend it is an exact quote?)

"Leverage is not just for carpenters or really old Greeks. You have probably benefited from the concept of leverage many times this week. If you've ridden an elevator, turned a screwdriver, or pedaled a bicycle, you've used leverage.

"And leverage is not just for physical objects. I recall, for example, Pat and Jerry, that you have a mortgage on your home. Most homebuyers don't pay cash. They go to a bank or mortgage broker to borrow money and make monthly payments which enable them to live in a house they probably could not afford if they had to pay cash.

"This is simply 'financial leverage.' And this is the way most homes as well as many businesses are financed. By using the financial leverage of a mortgage, a homeowner can live in a nice house while building equity through appreciation of the house value.

"There is a different type of financial leverage made available, not by mortgage brokers, but by *life insurance* brokers. If somebody is interested in creating a lump sum to be available upon an event like the death of a breadwinner, we can use the amazing innovation of LIFE INSURANCE to create that lump sum.

"And the leverage truly is amazing! If you are healthy, and especially if you are under age 80 and are a non-nicotine user, you can probably create an estate of $300,000, maybe even $500,000 or more using an annual or monthly payment for an affordable amount of money."

Rudi stopped long enough for a breath. Clearly he *loved* this subject. Pat smiled and urged him to continue. Which he happily did, leaning in toward the camera as he spoke. "Imagine for a moment that you are signing up for cryonic suspension immediately upon the pronouncement of legal death. We need to create a lump sum to pay for the cost of cryonic suspension, so let's use the figure of $200,000 that the Cryonics organization Alcor is currently charging for a full body suspension.

"Pat and Jerry, I know that you know this already, but there may be some folks, maybe really smart people who read books, who may want to understand this in a deeply meaningful way. What is the best way to create this $200,000 to go to Alcor?

"What if you happen to have $200,000 sitting under your pillow? Should you fund your preservation with this cash?"

Jerry shook his head. "I'm thinking there usually may be a better way, like the way we paid for our cryopreservations."

"Right on, Jerry. Almost certainly you won't want to spend that cash all up front. Let's just remind ourselves why. Let's take an example of a random client we'll call 'Joe' I just pulled from my desk file. He's 41 and reasonably healthy. Joe could have $200,000 of Index Universal Life coverage for $206 dollars a month, or $2,472 a year.

"It turns out if Joe funds his Cryonics with cash, Alcor needs the actual cash to be deposited with them, which they put in a safe but low interest bearing money market fund, at about 1% a year interest.

 "Is it reasonable to assume that over time Joe may average 5% a year with his $200,000 if it is invested somewhere else? I believe this is a pretty conservative interest assumption. So, Joe could be making about $10,000 a year by putting his

$200,000 in an index fund, instead of the $2,000 he would have if this money was sitting in a money market fund at Alcor. The difference of $8,000 is much higher than the actual COST of having the $200,000 of life insurance, which we recall is only about $2,500 a year!

"The interest gained on NOT paying cash is much higher than the cost of insurance!"

"We are completely with you on this," chimed in Jerry from the screen. "That's why we bought our Cryonics life insurance policies; the numbers made sense for us."

"They certainly do, Jerry, and it worked out especially well for you, since you are both in excellent health. To be fair, this will not always be the case. If a person is past age 80 or uninsurable because of health reasons, cash funding *may* make sense. But even in these situations, positioning the money in an annuity with a higher growth potential than with the Cryonics organization may be prudent. Better to keep your hard earned money working hard for you!

"But let's get back to our example with Joe, because I think this will make sense, given what we already know.

"Joe is looking at these numbers, and his choice is pretty obvious.

"He is further convinced of the rationality of life insurance because Joe has a wife and children he cares about. By using a life insurance policy to fund his Cryonics, the cost of cryopreservation is created exactly when needed and does not reduce the amount of his estate going to his family.

"Oh, and did we mention that this Index Universal Life policy Joe is funding for about $2,500 a year also grows an internal cash value, the part of the policy one does not need to 'die' to access? Joe's policy builds a tax-free, creditor-proof savings called the cash value of the policy. This cash value projects to over $133,000 at age 70, $377,000 at 85, and at age 100 over $962,000! All of these figures are *much* more than he has invested in the policy.

"The basic facts and simple math are why about 90% of people signed up for Cryonics currently use life insurance to pay for the cost of cryopreservation."

Jerry shifted in his seat so he and Pat were more centered on the screen and observed, "Yes, all this is pretty clear. But I think you mentioned that our programs are even better than we thought they were, and you used a phrase I've never heard of called a Life Insurance Retirement Plan. What's that all about?"

The LIRP: Life Insurance Retirement Plan

"I am so glad you asked," smiled Rudi. "And here is the good news. You two already own a Life Insurance Retirement Plan, happily called a LIRP! The Index Universal Life (IUL) policies you already own to fund your cryopreservation include a cash value that builds up - which you don't have to *die* to access. And we've talked about the fact that you can access the cash value of the policies by taking a zero interest loan using the cash value in the policy as collateral. This means you can access this money on a *tax-free* basis.

"Yes, I think we mostly understood this, Rudi," noted Pat, "but why are you now calling this a LIRP? I've never heard of this term. We wanted the policies to primarily be a way to pay the cost of cryopreservation. If we could pull a little bit of money out of them if we needed it, or maybe to supplement our retirement income, I guess that would be a plus, but it seems like this is kind of muddying the waters for what we want our policies to do. We both have 401k plans at work and we also fund our IRA plans to the extent we can. We're hoping that these 401k plans and our IRAs will provide a decent retirement income. Are you saying these aren't good programs?"

Using Life Insurance for Tax Benefits *Before* Cryopreservation

Rudi took a moment, looking thoughtful, trying to frame the best way to get a rather paradigm shifting concept across. Finally he spoke, a little slower and more deliberately paced than usual. "Let's take a minute and put the Cryonics piece aside, and just talk about tax benefits from your life insurance *before* cryopreservation.

"Let me be very clear about what we are talking about for the next few moments. . . the income tax benefits of your life insurance policies for retirement, while you are in this life, well before your 'dewar nap.' We are *not* discussing tax issues upon revival. That is a separate issue that I don't think anyone could reasonably discuss.

"I understand you both are successful professionals, Pat and Jerry. And, you'll recall we completed a financial fact-finder together when we established your earlier policies, and so of course I know you both are contributing to your 401k plans and your IRAs. And, these *are* good programs. And, *of course* you should contribute to your 401k to the extent that there are matching funds from your employer.

"And the Roth IRA that you have with me in the Variable Annuity is a *great* plan, and it will also contribute to your *tax-free* income when you start pulling money from your program. Of course you recognize there are limits with the

Roth, such as a fairly low maximum contribution, age requirements for access, and that many people cannot have a Roth because their income is reasonably high.

"That said, by the time you are ready to retire, it is very possible that tax rates may have increased considerably."

"Let's see if I'm getting your point here," Jerry interjected. "If future tax rates may be higher or possibly *much* higher, I see why we might even want to take some dollars we are currently putting into our 401k plans and IRA and redirect them to the Index Universal Life policies we have. I can see where that could be a benefit, since we can access the cash value in the IULs tax free."

"YES!" exclaimed Rudi. "Thank you for grasping this counterintuitive point. We'll need to do some actual investment runs to quantify this, but the bottom line is that it may well make sense to fund your 401k plans to the extent of the company match and then put the balance into your life insurance policies for income tax-free withdrawals.

"And, the reason this is also exactly on-point for our discussion is that you will want to have some additional policies dedicated to fund your Cryonics trust. And, if we direct the money you have been putting in your current 'eventually taxed plans' into the new 'won't EVER be income taxed plans,' you'll wind up with a double benefit!

"What would you think of this as a path forward? How about we fill out a new financial questionnaire for you to update the one we have on file, and together we'll find a way to comfortably and sustainably create an even better Life Insurance Retirement Plan for you?

"But let's get back to our example. Remember a few minutes ago we were talking about our cryonicist named Joe who used life insurance to fund his cryopreservation?"

Life Insurance Leverage Also Works for Cryonics Estate Planning!

"It turns out Joe was not just looking to fund his Cryonics, but wanted to fund a Cryonics Estate Plan as well. The exact same ideas apply. The leverage of life insurance still works.

"Our Joe is a pretty hard working and intelligent fellow, like most cryonicists. A few years after he signed up for Cryonics, he established a Cryonics Estate Plan, including a Personal Revival Trust™, through attorney Peggy Hoyt.

"And now he wants to have an EXTRA million dollars going into this trust when he 'dies.'

"Although Joe is a few years older, he finds the leverage of life insurance still works dramatically in his favor," Rudi enthused. "He finds he can create an extra MILLION dollars to fund his trust for about $13,000 a year. And, this still grows an internal cash value which projects at his age 100 to over $5 MILLION dollars!"

Jerry added, "Sounds like smart financial leverage!"

So Here Is the Take Home Story

"Most people who are signed up and properly funded for Cryonics are not mega-wealthy. They use the leverage of life insurance to handle their funding," Rudi reiterated.

"And, most people who have Cryonics Estate Plans with Personal Revival Trusts™ are not mega-wealthy. They *also* use the leverage of life insurance to fund their trusts.

"How great is that? The above facts may well mean that *you*, Jerry and Pat, (and lots of you, Dear Readers) may well be able to have and nicely fund a true Cryonics Estate Plan!

"I apologize to the two of you for doing way too much of the talking on this video conference, but I wanted to make sure that the benefits of using a life insurance policy to fund your Cryonics and your Cryonics Estate Plan are crystal clear. Questions or observations?"

While this had been a fairly lengthy explanation, and Jerry realized the time for this video call was drawing to a close, he wanted to make sure he understood the options available to him and Pat. "Let me get this straight, Rudi. We could buy a separate policy to fund our Cryonics trusts, I get that. But, even redirecting funds we've been putting into other retirement plans, I don't think we can afford a $13,000 a year premium for each of us, even if the policy does accumulate long range tax-free cash."

"Oh, I understand that!" Rudi responded quickly on the video screen. "That was simply an example. With your permission, since I already have all your health and biographical data, I will generate a full spreadsheet of choices you may want to consider. That $13,000 was for a full million of Index Universal Life just as an example."

"Would we have to qualify medically again?" asked Pat.

"Well, yes, but if nothing significant has changed since you two qualified a few years ago, this will not be a problem. And we have streamlined the application and underwriting process considerably. If you buy less than $1 million of coverage, we probably won't even need you to get blood and urine checkups."

"Well, you have certainly given us a lot to think about," said Pat, as a nice way of signaling the end of the videoconference. "Jerry and I are quite serious about making this happen, and now that we see we could afford to fund a Cryonics trust while still taking care of our family, I think we are closer to moving forward on this. Would you be kind enough, Rudi, to generate current quotes for each of us, starting with $100,000 of the Index Universal Life plan, and email them to us? And we need at least a week to discuss this privately, so let's set a follow up conference for maybe two weeks from tonight, same time?, if that time works for you, Jerry and Rudi?"

Rudi looked off camera at his calendar. "Perfect time for me!"

"And for me as well," added Jerry.

Getting ready to sign off, Rudi said, "Let me take a moment to say how much I like and respect you both for having the vision to pursue something as abstract and forward thinking as Cryonics Estate Planning. While there cannot be guarantees with this emerging science of Cryonics, it is looking increasingly credible. And, if Cryonics does indeed work, we all may be living some pretty amazing lifestyles as a direct result of what we've accomplished today. I look forward to talking again in two weeks! And meanwhile, I'll check in with Peggy Hoyt to see about setting up an introductory virtual meeting with you two."

Jerry said, "Great to see you again, Rudi...and by the way, I have a buddy at work who may be interested in Cryonics. I'll refer him to your website so you two can see if this is a fit."

Rudi gave an approving nod. "That is music to my ears! Would you do me a favor and send an introductory email to him and copy me, since sometimes people need a little nudge to get things rolling. I'll email Peggy now and send you some times that work for her. She is so popular, I know her schedule is really packed. And thanks again for calling!"

Chapter Four
Beginning the Cryonics Estate Planning Process

Rudi had emailed insurance quotes to Pat and Jerry soon after their video meeting, and following discussions with Rudi over the next two weeks, the couple were comfortable with the concept of increasing their life insurance leverage to fund their future. They were now anxious to meet Peggy Hoyt. Rudi assured them again that setting up an exploratory meeting with the attorney would not involve any cost or obligation on their part.

Rudi Arranges the Meeting With Peggy Hoyt

Pat and Jerry were eagerly looking forward to the video conference call and to discussing Cryonics Estate Planning options with Peggy. They clicked the link in the email Rudi had sent, and Rudi and Peggy appeared in their respective offices on a split screen.

"Good Morning, Jerry and Pat! Is the sound and video working okay for everyone? May I introduce Peggy Hoyt? Peggy, Jerry and Pat have been great clients for some time, and both are solidly funded with a dedicated life insurance policy for their Cryonics organization. As I was telling you earlier, Peggy, they are thinking about how to set up plans to protect their assets while alive, take care of their boys and pets if something happens to them, and figure out a way to be stone wealthy if Cryonics works and they are resuscitated in the future."

Jerry looked a little embarrassed at this slightly overblown introduction. "Nice to meet you, Ms. Hoyt. Actually, we don't need to be 'stone wealthy' in the future, but having some financial options would really be great. Pat and I are both in professional jobs, and we have noticed how quickly skill sets become obsolete. If we can afford to do it, we would like to put plans in place to have some kind of wealth available if and when we wake up from the long nap in that dewar at Alcor.

"But let me emphasize from the outset, Ms. Hoyt," he continued, "we aren't ready to commit to doing this right yet, and we have a lot of questions. Am I correct that this is a no cost or obligation meeting as Rudi implied?" Jerry said this with a smile to soften the content of his question.

Peggy returned the smile, looking directly at the camera as she said, "Yes, that is absolutely correct, Jerry. And please call me Peggy. Be assured that Rudi and I simply want to see if we can help, and there is exactly zero cost or obligation implied in this visit. Creating an estate plan is an investment of both time and money and we want to make sure this is the right time for you and that we are a good fit. If we decide to work together, that will be great. If we don't, that's okay too. I hope that answers your question, Jerry? And, by the way, Rudi said you two don't only love your kids and each other, but that you are crazy about your dogs. Sounds like you are interested in making sure that arrangements are made for them as well?"

Both Pat and Jerry responded to this, calling their dogs over to be in camera range, and an enthusiastic tail wagging pair came into view. There followed a good five minutes in which Pat and Jerry explained how they had come to adopt their rescue dogs, and how great the dogs were with the boys. Peggy explained that she has six dogs and two cats, as well as several horses at home. She went on to say that much of her practice involves planning for pets, horses, and other specialty situations, including persons with disabilities, elder law asset protection and non-traditional families. It quickly became clear that part of the DNA of the video call participants involved caring for both humans and non-humans!

This went on for what seemed a long time to Rudi, who said with a grin, "Well, friends, can we stipulate that we all love our pets? Including me! But, if it's okay, I think we have a hard stop on this call at the end of the hour, and I want to make sure we cover some business content here."

"Boo hiss!" called Pat, Jerry and Peggy. "We'd love to talk about our pets all day!" But this did provide the transition to business that they knew was needed.

"Peggy," began Pat, "Rudi was saying that you have done quite a few Cryonics Estate Plans using Personal Revival Trusts™?"

Rudi interrupted, "Peggy, I told them I believed that you and your team have set up more Cryonics Estate Plans than any other attorneys in the world!"

"There's no way to know for sure, but I have spent more than a decade working with cryonicists to accomplish their goals. And Rudi, I always appreciate your kind words and hearty recommendation," Peggy stated. "You know, Pat, that the number of folks signed up for Cryonics is not huge, and of those, only a small subset have so far executed Cryonics Estate Planning. But of *that* modest group, our team is helping a growing number of people. And, of course, while we have worked hard to develop a format and system to do this, every situation and every estate plan has unique considerations. Let's talk about your situation. You probably have some questions you've prepared?"

Getting the Logistical Questions Out of the Way

"Actually, we DID write down a few things we'd like to ask," Jerry said. "First, we live in California. I think Rudi said you are Florida based. Aren't lawyers subject to state specific regulations? How can you create an estate plan for us if you aren't in our state? Do you have an office here, Peggy? Or how would this work?"

"Good question, Jerry. Our firm is part of a nationwide network of estate planning attorneys. If you don't have an estate planning attorney you are currently working with, we can recommend one of the attorneys from our network to help prepare state specific legal directives. However, in some cases, our Cryonics clients find that a Florida based Cryonics estate plan meets their needs. Of course, the actual interviews with you are done just as we are doing now, over video conferencing systems like Zoom. Our team is used to working at a distance via phone and video calls. And with your professional backgrounds, I expect you are as well?"

"Absolutely. Thanks," said Pat. "So here's our next question. Let's say we set up a Personal Revival Trust™ and we fund it with an extra life insurance policy. When both Jerry and I are in the Cryonics dewar, who would manage this money? We love our boys, but they simply don't have the skill sets to manage money over extended periods of time."

Rudi chimed in. "I know Peggy will be answering this in greater detail over time, Pat and Jerry, but the short answer to the question is that this can be done by one or more institutional trustees. For example, we are currently working with Justin Cairns, Next Chapter Advisory Group, who is a Raymond James advisor. Fortunately, he happens to have an office about five minutes from Alcor in Scottsdale, AZ. Raymond James is a large, venerable financial institution willing to act as corporate trustee. And, this 'who is going to manage the money' question is as central and important as it gets, so we'll be talking about it a lot, along with the question of 'who watches over these trustees in a way that protects your long term interests?' Is that enough for now?"

Pat held up her hand in a Stop! signal. "Good short answer since we are just trying to get an overview today, and we'll definitely be revisiting the Trustee question with more specific questions later. It is reassuring to know you guys have thought about all this. So, what would need to happen next?"

So, How Do We Get Started? The Cryonics Decision Tree™

Peggy smiled as she answered, "So glad you asked, because we have designed a powerful tool to help us begin this process together." She held up some pages. "This is a planning tool we've designed called the Cryonics Decision Tree™ that helps us figure out together EXACTLY what is important to you, Pat and Jerry. Rudi said he'd sent you a copy of the *Cryonics Estate Planning Handbook?* The Decision Tree is **Appendix D**."

Pat held their *Handbook* up to the camera. "We have the book right here. Give us a minute to look at **Appendix D**." Pat flipped through the book, turning it so Jerry could read along. "Pretty cool – a Cryonics Decision Tree™! WOW! This is quite a few pages! You really DO have this down to a science! Just glancing at it, though, I think Jerry and I are going to need some time to consider how we both feel about these substantive questions."

Peggy was happy to respond to her concern. "The Cryonics Decision Tree™ may seem a little overwhelming and you may not know all the answers to the questions posed. That's okay, because we will work through each question to find the best result for you." Peggy grinned when she said, "Take your time, but hurry. Seriously, we just want to encourage you to keep the process moving."

The Next Step: The Discovery and Decision Dialogue™

"And just so you can get a feel for how we proceed," Peggy continued. "When you are ready, the next step will be to schedule another conference to discuss in detail the questions and concerns you've identified through the Cryonics Decision Tree™ process.

"We call that next meeting the Discovery and Decision Dialogue™. Essentially, you will teach *me* about you and your family; I will teach *you* about the law and how it affects your family. Then, together we can discuss the planning options that are available to meet your needs. After the meeting you will have some decisions to make. Is this the right time to do your planning? Are we a good fit as your law firm and advisor? And is the investment of time, money, and energy appropriate now? If we mutually decide this is a go, we'll proceed to develop a comprehensive Cryonics Estate Plan based upon your personal situation, your desires and ultimate goals."

There was a silence as everyone took time to absorb all the information that had been shared. Rudi broke the silence, giving a quick synopsis of the meeting and making sure everyone was comfortable with what had gone on and with what their next steps were going to be. "Great being with you all, and I look forward to our continuing interesting and productive relationship. Last thoughts, anyone? If not, let's put this videoconference in the win column."

Before signing off, Jerry added, "I am so pleased that there are actual structures in place we can follow! Peggy, it sounds like you offer a well-designed process and the thoughtful guidance we'll need to figure out exactly what we want to do. Thanks, everybody. I'm really looking forward to getting this put together!" After they closed the call, Jerry looked at his wife to get her reaction. "Well, I think that went pretty well. What do you think?"

Pat was enthusiastic. "I am really encouraged! This feels like a great direction for our family!"

Chapter Five
Does a Traditional Last Will and Testament Work for Cryonicists?

Pat and Jerry spent the next week working through the Cryonics Decision Tree™ process. They felt especially relieved to have all their assets identified and codified into a spreadsheet format. They confirmed ownership of all real property based on the actual title documents, reviewed the ownership of each of their financial accounts (oops, one checking account was only in Pat's name when they had thought it was jointly owned), and double checked that all the beneficiary designations on their existing retirement accounts (their 401ks and IRAs), annuities and life insurance policies were in line with their current plan.

When they felt ready, they contacted Peggy Hoyt who led them through the Discovery and Decision Dialogue™. With some further discussion, the three of them mutually agreed that this was the right time for Pat and Jerry to proceed with a serious Cryonics Estate Plan to augment their Cryonics intentions. They were ready to move forward with the design and implementation of their Cryonics Estate Plan.

General Considerations of Last Will and Testaments

Because Pat and Jerry were familiar with the concept of a Last Will and Testament, and had one for many years, Peggy suggested it might be a good place to begin their work together. "You may have heard the statement, 'If you don't have an estate plan, the law will create one for you,' " Peggy began. "For the cryonicist, any estate plan is better than not having one at all. The time to get started is now because tomorrow is the great unknown.

"No surprise, an essential component to every estate plan is a Last Will and Testament, (I'll just call it a Last Will for short)," she continued. "I know you are familiar with the format and concept, so I won't spend much time on those aspects. Just a few general things as reminders. . .

"First, asset ownership and beneficiary designations always trump the directions in your Last Will. Many people don't realize this and believe their Last Will is actually the last word. Unfortunately, as a result, sometimes estates plans don't work as intended.

"However, if you don't have a Last Will, then each state has a law, called the law of intestacy, that determines how your estate will be distributed.

"One misconception is that if you don't have a Last Will, the state where you live will take your estate. This is not true in most cases because the law of intestacy will actually determine who is entitled to your estate. Your beneficiaries will be your heirs, that is, the persons who are most closely related to you. The state only becomes your heir if you die without any relatives. Check out **Appendix E**, the Table of Consanguinity, in your Handbook if you want to see how the relationships are typically tiered.

"A Last Will does a couple of really important things. It allows you to nominate a Personal Representative or Executor to be responsible for the administration of your estate. This person is charged with the responsibility of identifying all of your probate assets, notifying and paying creditors and final taxes and then distributing the remaining assets to your named beneficiaries. If you have minor children, your Last Will also nominates the guardians who will become responsible for raising your children and the trustees who will be managing their assets."

Naming Your Personal Representative and Guardian

"The person you choose as your Personal Representative should be someone who is responsible and will carry out your wishes. This person should be someone you trust implicitly, who is organized, and who has knowledge of your Cryonics goals. In addition, make sure you choose someone over the age of 18, who isn't a felon, and who meets the requirements for your State. In Florida, only relatives or Florida residents who meet the other criteria are eligible to serve as Personal Representative.

"The person or persons you choose as Guardian for your minor children will likely be a family member who shares your family goals and values. However, in some cases, you may want to choose a trusted family friend. These will be the people who are going to raise your children if you are unable to do so."

Pat smiled as she nudged her husband and quipped, "Jerry, we surely must know someone we trust who is not a career criminal and felon. If not, we'll have to start hanging with a better class of people."

Executing Your Last Will and Testament

Peggy continued, smiling at Pat's sense of humor, "Your Last Will must be executed with certain formalities to be legal. This is where a do-it-yourselfer might get in trouble. Signing a piece of paper and dating it likely won't work. Most Last Wills require, at a minimum, a signature, a date, and multiple witnesses. In some states, a Last Will needs to be signed a second time in the presence of the same witnesses and in the presence of a notary (who can't be one of the witnesses). This second verification is called a Self-Proving Affidavit. Without it, there can be delays in getting your Last Will admitted to probate. For the cryonicist, delays can mean trouble, and in all likelihood permanent and irreversible death.

"Without these formalities and in the absence of a valid Last Will, your assets may not be distributed the way you had intended, but instead may be distributed to your 'heirs at law' according to the laws of intestacy. Usually, these are the people who are your closest relatives at the time of your legal death and they will undoubtedly be pleased you left them a nice inheritance!"

"Amazing how many relatives you didn't know you had pop out after a death, isn't it?" Jerry remarked with a smirk.

"We've all seen that happen," Peggy agreed. "Still, for some people in some circumstances, a Last Will can be the appropriate vehicle to communicate their wishes for what happens to their personal and financial assets at the time of their legal death. Here's the hitch: not every estate plan should use a Last Will as the primary set of instructions, because of the inherent disadvantages of that tool. If you choose to use a Last Will as your only planning tool, there may be some problematic consequences."

And Then, There's Probate

"A Last Will and Testament requires a court ordered administration, known affectionately, as you are undoubtedly aware, as probate. Wills REQUIRE probate. For emphasis, let me say it again, a Last Will REQUIRES probate. No way around it. This may come as a shock, but it is definitely true.

"Probate, you recall, is the formal process where the Court establishes the validity of a deceased person's Last Will. The Probate Court will appoint your Personal Representative or Executor for the purposes of identifying and valuing the assets of your estate, paying your final creditors, and delivering the balance of your assets to your heirs.

"Probate can take months and, in some cases, years, depending on the complexity of the assets. It can also depend on whether there are challenges from heirs and/or complications related to creditors."

"That happened when my brother-in-law died," Pat interjected. "It seemed like forever before the family was able to sell his house or get all his bills taken care of. It was terrible for everybody!"

Peggy nodded. "That's a good example why for many people probate is a four letter word! Judges are unpredictable. Court dockets are crowded. Family members can be unreliable. We should probably also mention that probate can offer disgruntled heirs a forum for challenging the provisions in your Last Will. Even if you include one of those 'no contest' clauses in order to keep people from challenging your Last Will, they aren't always effective and in many states, with

Florida as a prime example, they aren't even recognized as valid. (By the way, however, a no contest clause is still a great idea and I definitely recommend including one!)

"There clearly are issues with a traditional Last Will and Testament. You can see why cryonicists may choose to avoid these risks by looking at other options."

A Fundamental Decision for Your Cryonics Estate Plan: A Last Will Only OR a Living Trust with a Pour-Over Will as Your Primary Planning Tool?

"Okay, we see that probate can be time-consuming depending on the laws of your state, and it certainly has a cost and is a public process with judicial oversight," observed Jerry from the screen.

Peggy paused and looked directly into the camera. "So now let's say for argument's sake you want to AVOID probate because you aren't too crazy about the delay, the cost or the judicial oversight.

"There is a way we can combine the benefits of a Living Trust, that lovely legal vehicle that avoids probate, with a special kind of Last Will, called a Pour-Over Will. Let's see how this might fit your needs."

Chapter Six
Your Cryonics Friendly Living Trust With Your Personal Revival Trust™
(Oh, and Your Pour-Over Will)

Pat, Jerry, and Peggy took breaks for coffee and treats in their respective locations. "How are you feeling about this so far?" Peggy asked when they all returned to their computer screens.

"I think we're ready to learn more about the possibility of creating a trust, since you've made some of the limitations of only having a Last Will and Testament pretty clear," Pat answered for the couple.

"Perfect. As committed cryonicists, you'll definitely want to explore all of the options available for a trust-based plan. Essentially, you'll want a Living Trust you can use during your lifetime *and* that will provide you with protection in the event of your mental or physical disability. And then, after your legal death, this directive will create a legal structure for the growth and maintenance of your financial assets for your future Revival. We call the Living Trust that accomplishes all of these goals a Personal Revival Trust™ (PRT™)."

"But let's not get ahead of ourselves," Peggy continued. "Shall we start with a quick overview of some basic definitions and general advantages of Living Trusts, just to make sure we are all on the same page? And then we can talk about why a Living Trust can be particularly beneficial for cryonicists."

So What IS a Living Trust?

"Trusts can appear complex, but they are essentially legal contracts where the Trustmaker, the Trustee and the Beneficiary are *all* initially the same person, which happens to be YOU, as the creator of the trust! Pretty cool, huh?

"Yes, you are the CREATOR of the Trust (sometimes also referred to as Settlor, Grantor, Trustor or Trustmaker). You are also the TRUSTEE in charge of managing the trust assets while you are alive and well. If you become unable to meaningfully participate in your legal and financial decisions during your lifetime due to illness or mental disability, you'll have a successor Trustee, but until your legal death, you are also the PRIMARY BENEFICIARY of the Trust.

"You recall that when we talked about how a Last Will works, with some exceptions, your possessions or properties are subject to probate. The main idea of a Living Trust is to make your Living Trust the 'owner' of some or all of your assets, so those assets are *not* subject to probate or to certain taxes or fees.

"Like any good contract, the terms of the contract control the operation of the Trust and provide guidance for future successor Trustees when you are no longer acting as trustee.

"Let me do a screen share so you can check out this list of benefits of Living Trusts in general."

Benefits of Living Trusts

There are many benefits of Living Trusts, some of which include:
- The terms of the Living Trust are private. Since they do not require probate – a public process with the oversight of a judge – the Living Trust should never be recorded in any public records.
- They can include specific provisions for determining whether you are mentally disabled and avoid a "forced guardianship" or court ordered disability determination.
- They can provide for one or more successor Trustees to take care of you and your loved ones if you are unable to act as Trustee.
- At your legal death, your trust can provide for your spouse, children or pets in a protected irrevocable trust and then remaining trust assets can be "transferred" to the Personal Revival Trust™ after the lifetimes of these beneficiaries. The benefit of keeping assets in an irrevocable trust for your beneficiaries is to create protections for both the assets and the

beneficiaries. The most common types of protection would be protection from themselves (in the event of minority, disability or inability to manage assets), divorce protection (affectionately referred to as "Biff and Bambi" protection), creditor protection (from catastrophic financial events like lawsuits or bankruptcy) and disability protections (from catastrophic health events).
- There are no lifetime gift tax implications for the transfer of assets to a Living Trust.
- Pets can be protected through the use of a Pet Trust.
- At legal death, if estate taxes are a concern, legal structures can be created to help to avoid or minimize estate taxes.
- Trusts are more difficult to contest than a Last Will and Testament. Trusts can also include "no contest" or "in terrorem" provisions to discourage litigation of the trust terms.

After they read through the list together, Pat shook her head and observed, "Peggy, I'm beginning to understand why you have been suggesting that a trust might be a more robust tool for our estate planning than just a Last Will and Testament! Impressive differences!"

Jerry added, "But aren't there lots of different kinds of trusts? What would be the best kind for us when we are committed to Cryonics?"

"You've been doing your homework, Jerry," Peggy answered. "Fortunately, Rudi and I and a serious group of estate planners have been working on these issues for several decades. And one part of the answer is that you might actually have *more* than one type of trust, depending on your unique needs and planning objectives.

"Since we are screen sharing, here's a document that might be useful at this point. It shows critical aspects of the different kinds of trusts."

Types of Trusts

Trusts Can Be Revocable Trusts or Irrevocable Trusts

That means just what those words imply:

Revocable: A Revocable Trust can be changed or amended during your lifetime. In addition, you can take assets out of the trust, put more assets in, or even retract the trust. This type of trust is sometimes referred to as a Revocable Living Trust or Living Trust, since it was created by the Trustmaker during their lifetime and exists as long as the Trustmaker is living.

Peggy interrupted their reading to quip, "And if you like Latin and want to win on Jeopardy, just remember this type is also referred to as an '*inter vivos*' trust."

Irrevocable: Irrevocable Trusts can also be created during the Trustmaker's lifetime but generally cannot be amended or changed after creation, except by court order or under the direction of a Trust Protector. Standalone Irrevocable Trusts can be created and funded for many purposes, including gifting, asset protection from claims of creditors, long term care asset protection (for government benefits eligibility like Medicaid), special needs planning and the minimization of estate taxes, to name a few.

Trusts Can Be Living Trusts or Testamentary Trusts

Living Trusts: A Living Trust is created during the Trustmaker's lifetime and exists as long as the Trustmaker is living. It includes instructions that are valid while you are alive, in the event of your mental disability and ultimately, upon your legal death. For the cryonicist, the Living Trust also contemplates the future Revival of the Trustmaker through the use of a Personal Revival Trust™.

Testamentary Trusts: A Testamentary Trust doesn't exist (except in concept) until your legal death. Testamentary trusts are generally irrevocable and provide instructions detailing how trust assets are to be utilized. A Testamentary Trust (of which the Personal Revival Trust™ is a special case) is created either as a sub-trust in a Last Will (not recommended for cryonicists, because of probate) or as part of a Living Trust (preferred for the Personal Revival Trust™ since it can then avoid issues related to the probate process).

Trusts Can Be Created to Benefit Multiple Generations

Dynasty Trusts: A Dynasty Trust is intended to last for an indefinite period of time (but not longer than the Rule Against Perpetuities) for the benefit of persons who are not yet alive and are therefore "unknown," but who are entitled to the distribution of the trust assets in the future.

Dynasty Trusts are subject to the Rule Against Perpetuities, known commonly as RAP. The RAP essentially says that a trust cannot have an unlimited life; it must end at some date in the future and the assets held by the Dynasty Trust must be distributed to the beneficiaries. Some states have abolished the Rule Against Perpetuities or have significantly extended the time period.

"Interesting!" Pat said. "That whole 'Is it even possible to have any control of what happens in the future?' element was a huge factor for Jerry and me before we even contacted you. Our conversation with Rudi on the very subject of Dynasty

Trusts – that they have been around and effective and *legal* for a long time – really helped us make our decision to move forward with this estate plan."

"I'm sure Rudi emphasized that many states have abolished the RAP, meaning essentially that trusts in those states can last forever," Peggy responded. "And other states have extended the RAP for extremely long periods of time. You can check out **Appendix F** of the *Handbook* for a chart of the RAP provisions by State.

"So now let's see where the Personal Revival Trust™ we could create for you fits into these different types of trusts."

Your Personal Revival Trust™

"To meet the unique challenges of setting up estate plans for cryonicists, over the years our firm has created and refined the Personal Revival Trust™," Peggy stated. "Where do you think it fits with the types of trusts we've just read about?"

"Based on what you've told us, Peggy," Jerry quickly responded, "I'd say your PRT™ is a form of a Dynasty Trust, which can last a long time and be available to us upon Revival."

"And," Pat jumped in, "what I hear you saying is that a Personal Revival Trust™ will be created as a Living Trust during our lifetime and then after our legal death becomes an irrevocable Dynasty Trust. So, how did we do, Peggy?"

"Right on, both of you! Yes, a PRT™ is a form of Living Trust that provides for you and your loved ones during your lifetime AND can also provide for you and your family after your legal death. For simplicity, Rudi and I have gotten in the habit of referring to a Living Trust as a PRT™ because they are specifically drafted and designed for the unique needs of the cryonicist.

"The primary purpose of the PRT™ is to provide the cryonicist, you, access to your financial resources at the time of your Revival, and as a result, a PRT™ is, indeed, a form of Dynasty Trust.

"But now," Peggy said in a more serious tone, "a reality check. Although Dynasty Trusts are designed to benefit multiple generations of people or charitable interests and have been around for as long as trusts have existed, the concept of the Personal Revival Trust™ is relatively new. The PRT™ concept has never been tested, because no one who has ever created a PRT™ has yet been revived from cryopreservation.

"Given that reality, let me share a bit about the concepts behind the PRT™. There's an old saying, 'Pigs get fat and hogs get slaughtered.' The context of that phrase relates to what happens when planning techniques are stretched to limits that walk the thin line between valid and overreaching. Given that we cannot predict the future with 100% certainty, a fairly conservative approach to the long-term maintenance and preservation of your Personal Revival Trust™ seems warranted.

"A conservative approach might suggest a portion of the PRT™ assets be paid periodically to an identifiable beneficiary. This beneficiary could be an individual (ultimately problematic because any named individual will have a specific and ultimately, finite life expectancy) or an organization (that theoretically has an unlimited life). In many cases, clients have chosen to pay a portion of the annual PRT™ income to the Cryonics organization where they intend to be suspended and/or to other scientific organizations that are working toward the creation of technologies that could ensure future Revival."

Intrigued, Jerry couldn't help but wonder, "Does the payment of income or principal to a person or organization guarantee the PRT™ will be recognized as a legitimate trust decades into the future?"

"There is no way to know for sure," Peggy explained, "but best practices dictate that planning contemplates the laws we are aware of today and then provides mechanisms (like a Trust Protector) for amendment and revision as laws change in the future."

"Got it…makes sense…please go on," observed Jerry.

"Personal Revival Trust™ instruments are revocable and can be modified anytime up to the time the Trustmaker dies or becomes incompetent. After legal death, the PRT™ will be irrevocable and may only be modified or changed by the court or through a Trust Protector with the power to modify the trust terms.

"Well, Jerry and Pat, fun stuff, eh? To clear our minds with a simpler subject, why don't we quickly go over the Pour-Over Will that will become part of your Cryonics Estate Plan, assuming you continue to favor having a Living Trust rather than a Last Will and Testament as your primary estate vehicle."

And Your Pour-Over Will

"You two have proven that you are fast learners and generally brilliant, so just a quick review of things I believe you already understand: A trust only controls property titled and held in the name of the trust. (The process of changing the title of assets into the name of the trust is called 'funding' or 'asset integration.')

"Any assets that are held in an individual's name; any assets that are titled as 'joint tenants with rights of survivorship' (like you confirmed your home is, Pat and Jerry); or any assets that have beneficiary designations naming individuals (like your

Jackson IRA you wrote through Rudi, Jerry, that names your two sons as beneficiaries) are **NOT** controlled by the trust and its terms. And no amount of 'wishing' this were different changes the outcome! These assets will be delivered directly to the co-owner or beneficiary.

"So, if those things are taken care of, why do you still need a Pour-Over Will? A Pour-Over Will is a legal directive that transfers any remaining probate assets to your Trust upon declaration of your legal death. I like to affectionately refer to the Pour-Over Will as a 'legal pooper scooper,' because its job is to make sure that all assets owned by you are ultimately part of your PRT™. It is not uncommon for someone to accidentally overlook a bank account or other property and the Pour-Over Will solves potential problems like that.

"What questions do you have, Pat and Jerry? What are you thinking?"

"Everything we've talked about today makes sense to me," Jerry answered. "And since you already have so much of our information, thanks to our Cryonics Decision Tree™ and the Discovery and Decision Dialogue™, I'd be comfortable moving on to phase two, the PRT™ Design Meeting. What do you think, Pat?"

"I'm right with you, Jerry. But Peggy, I do have one question before we go further. You've mentioned a Trust Protector several times. Can you elaborate on that role?"

"Hah, the Trust Protector - yes - just what the heck is a Trust Protector? How about if we talk about that important role right after we all take a quick break? I'll meet you back in ten minutes."

Chapter Seven
Time Out Again!
What's the Deal With Trustees and Trust Protectors?

"Okay, it is time for some clarification," Peggy began when they were all reassembled in front of their respective screens. "Pat, you are right: I've mentioned the concept of Trustees and Trust Protectors a number of times and we do need to take a step back to see what they do, why they do it, and how it impacts your Cryonics Estate Plan.

"How about if we start with the role of Trustee, since that is the position most people are familiar with?"

The Role of Trustee

Peggy began the explanations. "A Trustee can be an individual or a couple of individuals, a professional like an attorney or certified public accountant, or a corporation such as a bank, trust company, or charity qualified to act as a Trustee.

"A Trustee's functions are to be responsible for the day-to-day management of the trust assets, to adhere to the terms of the trust for the benefit of the beneficiaries, to carry out the intent of the Trustmaker, and to deliver the remaining Trust assets to the final beneficiary when the terms of the Trust are complete.

"That's probably an over-simplification, but it gives you the idea that 'Trustee' is a pretty important role! It's not one that you should grant lightly without considering all of the possibilities and options! A Trustee serves in a fiduciary role, which is a serious position of trust. So naturally, the person(s) or organizations you choose should be trustworthy."

"No kidding, that's some heavy duty responsibilities!" Jerry piped in.

Special Challenges in Identifying Trustees for Cryonicists

"Ultimately," Peggy continued, "You'll want a corporate Trustee for the time you are in cryopreservation - mostly, because it could be a really long time and humans just don't live that long.

"Corporations, on the other hand, can theoretically live forever. But even corporations don't tend to stay the same and this is especially true in the banking industry, as the big banks continuously eat up the little banks, we have a financial crisis, and banks go out of business, yada, yada, you get the idea. Even trust companies that could once boast they had been in business for more than 100 years have been taken over by other organizations."

Pat and Jerry looked at each other with concern.

Catching the look, Peggy quickly said, "Hang on, friends. All is not lost. Strangely, that's the GOOD news! Even if the bank or trust company you choose gets merged into another entity, it will likely STILL exist in some form. Plus, the laws surrounding trust companies are not the same as those for banks. Trust companies can't take your deposits and then loan them out. They have to actually have your funds on reserve in case you want them back.

"A bit of history? The challenge we've faced with Cryonics Estate Planning and Personal Revival Trusts™ is finding corporate Trustees who are willing to learn about the world of Cryonics and what it might mean for them as a business model. Several banks have said they were interested and then backed out because the science isn't proven or they think Cryonics will cast a bad shadow on their reputation.

"It's funny," Peggy mused. "While the trust companies seem to want to manage the money, they just don't want to have anything to do with making sure their 'cryo-beneficiary' is still in a preserved state.

"Doesn't make any sense to us." Peggy grinned. "Seems like cryonicists would be the ideal beneficiary. They never call you; they never ask you for money; they never make your life difficult! All you have to do is manage their money, watch it double, triple, quadruple, etc., for a number of years and periodically check in to make sure their dewar is still intact and they haven't been revived!

"Enough history, because now, fortunately, times are changing! Today, we are finally working with a number of organizations that seem to really 'get it.'

"So, that's the Trustee. Let's look at how that compares to the Trust Protector role and then we can take some time for your questions."

So, Just What the Heck Is a Trust Protector?

"Here's where the whole concept of the Trust Protector becomes important. A Trust Protector is also a fiduciary (although this concept is often open for debate) but they aren't the Trustee and they aren't the beneficiary of the trust they are appointed to protect.

"A Trust Protector is an independent third party (or panel of people) who can act on behalf of an Irrevocable Trust for the purpose of carrying out duties related to the trust. The Trust Protector is empowered to do things the Trustee can't do, shouldn't do or doesn't want to do. Typically the Trust

Protector is given multiple powers, for example to amend the trust in the event of changed circumstances, to review trust accountings, to remove and replace Trustees when appropriate, and to correct scrivener's errors. In one sense, the job of the Trust Protector is to make sure the trust stays viable and that the Trustee is doing their job."

Identifying Your Cryonics Friendly Trust Protector

"A Trust Protector, just like your Trustee, should be a person or organization who is friendly to your Cryonics adventure, who will ideally ensure your assets are available when you reanimate."

Pat and Jerry nodded and signaled for Peggy to continue. "In the Cryonics context, the Trust Protector is empowered to do some additional chores. The Trust Protector is charged with the responsibility of making sure the cryo-beneficiary (you) is still happily cryopreserved. The Trust Protector then reports this information back to the Trustee so they know they have a job for a while longer. The Trust Protector will also be charged with the responsibility of letting the Trustee know when you've been revived and that they can now distribute the trust assets to the new and improved, revived *you*. You may also want to empower your Trust Protector to review annual accountings prepared by the Trustee to make sure they are being 'prudent' with your assets.

"Since Trust Protectors are usually people, this is where finding volunteers might get a little tricky. However, there are great minds in the Cryonics world working on this one. There's a group of young cryonicists referred to as the Teens and Twenties who have expressed an interest in supporting their more senior counterparts as they head off into the 'great dewar in the sky.'"

Teens and Twenties of Cryonics

Peggy described this amazing group: "This 'Teens and Twenties of Cryonics' group has been gathering annually since 2007. Bill Faloon, the CEO of the Life Extension Foundation, pays the cost for about 50 of the brightest and most dedicated fully signed and funded cryonicists under age 30 to come to this remarkable meeting.

"From this group, and a related group of cryonicists called the 'Asset Preservation Group,' we have identified a number of highly ethical, dedicated, and brilliant younger people willing and able to serve in the role of Trust Protector.

"We've also been asking cryopreservation organizations like Alcor, The Cryonics Institute, and the American Cryonics Society to appoint persons they feel are willing to competently and enthusiastically carry out this responsibility. You can, of course, initially appoint anyone you want as your Trust Protector. But, understand, at some point there is going to have to be a mechanism to make sure future Trust Protectors are also appointed.

"A Trust Protector has been essential to getting the trust companies to agree to serve on behalf of Personal Revival Trusts™. The trust companies really do not want any responsibility when it comes to the verification of the continued cryopreservation of the beneficiary and then, ultimately, their revival. In fact, some of them want very little responsibility other than simply managing the money."

"Wow! The job of Trust Protector seems like it really is an important role. I'm guessing, but I would assume that most Trust Protectors don't take on all this responsibility for free?" Jerry wondered.

"Great point, Jerry, and very astute of you," Peggy responded. "Both Trustees and Trust Protectors will expect to be paid for the services they provide. For Trustees, their fees are generally a percentage multiplied by the total value of the assets under their management. Typically, the more money you have, the lower the overall percentage. For example, trusts up to $1,000,000 might be at a higher percentage rate than trusts with more than $1,000,000. You can generally expect fees to be in the 1% to 2.5% range depending on the size of your estate. This is an annual fee and will vary based on the growth of the assets.

"And, that brings up another potential challenge. Many banks and trust companies have minimum investment requirements. Our experience is that the larger companies want at least $1,000,000 of assets under management. As a result, we've been working hard to find a trust company that will accept smaller trusts. And, remember, this amount can include Life Insurance proceeds. So, let's say you have a net worth, including your home, of $500,000. You could add a $500,000 life insurance policy, and the global amount in the trust would meet this $1,000,000 minimum. Stay tuned for more information in the future!

"Trust Protectors generally don't charge a percentage of the assets. Depending on whether they are individuals or an organization, they might choose to charge on an hourly basis or reduced percentage rate, depending on their actual duties and the amount of time they spend taking care of business. And typically, a Trust Protector would not have a minimum asset size requirement."

"We can see these are both very important roles," Pat remarked on behalf of the couple. "Thanks for sharing that information, because it gives us even more to think about. Peggy, any other big issues we need to be aware of as we start to get all this down on paper?"

"Well, actually, so glad you asked, because I think we need to discuss one more big concern that will inform your decisions. When you are ready, let's tackle guardianship."

Chapter Eight
Cryonicists Need to Avoid Forced Guardianship.
Let's Talk About How to Do That!

After getting a nod from Pat, Jerry gave a thumbs up to Peggy. "We are definitely ready to hear any information that will help us make good long-term decisions!"

"Well, moving along then," Peggy began again, "no estate plan is complete without a full complement of 'disability directives,' those legal instruments that empower agents or 'attorneys-in-fact' to act on your behalf should you no longer have the capacity to act on your own behalf.

"Your physical or mental health can change in an instant - and, as the saying goes, 'Life happens fast!' If there is ever a time when you aren't able to make your own decisions, your estate planning directives become the most important legal instruments you can have.

"The problem is, most people wait too long. We assume our good health is going to last indefinitely. Unfortunately, it does not! Without a strong disability plan, you are up the proverbial creek, which likely would take the form of a forced guardianship.

"Not to belabor the point, but let's get guardianship out of the way so we can discuss all of the ways to avoid it! In its simplest form, a guardianship is a lawsuit your family or loved ones file against you; you get to pay for it; and you lose."

"I already don't like where this guardianship thing is going!" Pat sighed.

Why Guardianship Is a Particular Problem for Cryonicists

"And once you've lost," Peggy continued, "a judge will make the final determination as to your competency and then appoint your guardian, the person who is legally authorized to act on your behalf. You officially become 'the ward.' This is likely where the phrase 'ward of the state' came from, because now all of your delegated activities are monitored by a state agency, the court system.

"If you had really, really, really 'good intentions' but never got around to actually completing your Cryonics application, funding it with life insurance, and finalizing your Cryonics Estate Plan, and you then become disabled, your Cryonics goal may never be realized.

"The only way a Cryonics plan could be implemented after a determination of incapacity and the appointment of a guardian would be to petition the guardianship court for authorization. This would entail additional costs and substantial uncertainty.

"And to make your plans successful, under a guardianship a judge would have to grant your guardian permission to enter into a cryopreservation contract on your behalf, allow it to be paid for from your resources, and then grant permission for the creation and transfer of assets to a Personal Revival Trust™. If you got a judge who is unenthusiastic about Cryonics, your plans for Revival in the future would be lost. There just aren't any guarantees, and it isn't worth the risk when proper planning can *prevent* this kind of unwanted outcome.

"Here's a PDF I can email you with some additional basic information about guardianships." Peggy shared a document on her screen and then forwarded a copy to Pat and Jerry.

General Information on Guardianships

The guardianship process is controlled by state guardianship laws and is sometimes referred to as "living probate," since the process provides for the management of the ward's assets and creditors while a person is living but in an incapacitated state.

The guardianship process examines the mental capacity of the alleged incapacitated person (AIP) and if that person is found to be incompetent (also known as incapacitated), a judge appoints a guardian to act on their behalf.

A guardianship can be for financial matters only, for personal matters only, or for both personal and financial matters (called a plenary guardianship).

Guardianship proceedings involve 3 factors:
1. **Determination of mental incapacity.** Guardianship requires the production of medical evidence of the AIP's mental incapacity. The law generally requires the level of proof be "clear and convincing" evidence or some other appropriate level. The courts are reluctant to take away a person's autonomy and legal rights. Therefore, the level of proof is sufficiently high to confine court intervention to serious situations. The AIP is required to be represented by legal counsel and is entitled to "due process" that includes being kept apprised of all of the relevant activities of the proceeding, including notice of all hearings and an opportunity to be present. Once the determination of incapacity has been made, a guardian will be appointed. The guardian will either have full or limited powers, depending on the severity of the incapacity.
2. **Appointment of a guardian and the granting of authority over the ward's person and/or the ward's**

property. The court will determine who should be appointed as the legal guardian of the deemed incapacitated person, now referred to as the ward. The person who is selected as the legal guardian will be based on the facts and circumstances of the case, as well as on state law. State statutes set forth the hierarchy of persons eligible to serve as a guardian. Usually, your guardian would be your spouse, then your adult children, then more remote relatives. **It's important to point out here that a lifelong partner to whom you are not married would be considered a stranger and not even on the list of eligible guardians.** And, if no one is willing or able to assume the role of guardian, the court may be forced to appoint a professional guardian.

The court has the authority to divide the responsibilities of the guardian into two different roles; one is guardian "over the person" and the other is guardian "over the property or estate" of the incapacitated ward. This means that a family member might be named as the guardian over the physical well-being of the ward but an accountant or professional guardian might be named to handle the financial affairs. This division of responsibilities is likely to occur where the court has some concern that a family member lacks sophistication, might exploit the ward, or might be exploited by others if placed in charge of the ward's finances. Most contested guardianships involve fights over who will be appointed as guardian of the property.

3. **Accounting to the court regarding the ward's affairs.** Regular accounting reports must be given to the court to permit the judge to review and supervise the guardian's activities. Expenditures from the ward's assets must comply with specific standards and the court reviews all accounts on a regular basis, typically bi-annually or annually. Failure to comply with the standards required by the court can be grounds for sanctions, including removal of the guardian.

   The guardian typically receives reasonable compensation for handling the ward's affairs, also subject to court approval. Guardians may be required to secure a bond (like an insurance policy) to cover losses to the ward's financial accounts due to the guardian's fault or neglect.

If the ward regains their mental capacity, the ward will need to produce medical proof of this fact and convince the court to return the authority to handle their own affairs. As you might expect, reversing the guardianship process comes with its own challenges and obstacles.

Having scanned the PDF document together, Jerry noted, "As you may have suspected, Peggy, Pat and I are both kind of 'control freaks.' Guardianship sounds exactly like a situation we *absolutely* want to avoid!"

"You and Pat are in good company, Jerry. Just to make my point crystal clear, the enthusiastic cryonicist NEVER wants to end up as a ward (better known as a victim!) in a guardianship proceeding. There is way too much uncertainty on outcomes related to the management of assets and pursuing the goals of cryopreservation at the time of legal death. For the cryonicist, a guardianship may be the worst kind of lawsuit you could experience."

"So what are the best ways we can make sure WE stay in control?" Pat asked.

How to Avoid the Dreaded Guardianship!

"The best advice, Pat, especially for cryonicists, is to pre-emptively do everything you can to avoid a court ordered guardianship!

"If you want to make sure your cryonic suspension, your Cryonics Estate Plan, and the proper funding of your plan are realized, then YOU must be the person who implements that plan while you have the mental capacity to do so. Proper pre-planning for your personal cryopreservation and the preservation of your assets is essential."

A Well Documented and Comprehensive Cryonics Estate Plan

"We can assume you two are more proactive than just waiting around for some shoe to drop, since you are here actually creating your Cryonics Estate Plan – not just talking about it. Each element of the Plan that we prepare together plays a part in avoiding guardianship.

"It's no accident that your Cryonics Estate Plan also includes documentation for a Pre-Need Guardian Declaration, which you can read about in Chapter Eight in the *Handbook* and for the other powerful tools we employ: the Durable Financial Power of Attorney, covered in Chapter Nine; Durable Healthcare Power of Attorney, in Chapter Ten; Living Will, Chapter Twelve; and Religious Objection to Autopsy, Chapter Thirteen. For the cryonicist, each of these disability directives needs to be carefully crafted for your specific situation and concerns."

A Pre-Need Guardian Declaration

"The best way to avoid having someone appointed as your guardian that you don't want or don't know is to **proactively nominate a guardian for yourself by creating a Pre-Need Guardian Declaration.** This Declaration is a directive that reflects your selection of a guardian and is only relevant in the event your other disability directives are ineffective or absent and there is an official proceeding that determines your incapacity.

"A pre-need guardian is kind of like 'a sweater in a suitcase.' You don't need it at the time it is created, but like that extra sweater you packed for unpredictable weather, it sure is nice to have it when you need it. The Pre-Need Guardian Declaration 'stands by' and is not used unless and until there is a guardianship proceeding. In most cases, it is never used at all, but that doesn't mean it isn't important.

"As mentioned earlier, in the absence of a pre-need nomination of your preference for the appointment of a guardian, state statutes will control the priority and selection of that person. These statutes generally favor family members including spouses, adult children, siblings and even remote family members. Disclaimer: Your directive will be instructive and persuasive to the court, but the judge is not bound by your nomination of guardian because there are many other factors that could also be considered.

"You can name different people for the guardian of the person and guardian of the property components. And nominating a Cryonics friendly guardian is critical for you as cryonicists, Pat and Jerry. Although a guardian is charged with making decisions consistent with how you, as the ward, would make them, there is no guarantee a judge would authorize or require a guardian to carry out your Cryonics preservation goals.

"So, in our practice we refer to this instrument as a 'fail safe' directive. If all else fails, then this directive is your last resort to control a process over which you potentially have no control. Really important stuff for cryonicists!"

Pat nodded. "Since I'm always cold, I found your 'sweater in a suitcase' idea even more compelling than your 'fail safe' reference, Peggy. But either analogy makes this Pre-Need Guardian Declaration something I don't want to be without! Seriously, is there anything else we can do to avoid the dreaded guardianship?"

Your Living Trust:
Financial and Healthcare Directives on Steroids

"Well, here's the biggee!" Peggy answered. "The great news? *Trusts* can do even more than we gave them credit for before!"

"You recall trusts are usually discussed in terms of 'death planning,' since there are so many advantages to the use of trusts for the long term management of assets into the future. But, what is NOT talked about as often is the power trusts offer in the context of disability planning!

"Well designed trusts have the potential to help you avoid guardianship proceedings, to keep your healthcare and financial matters private, and to permit you the ability to name those you love (or at least trust and have confidence in) to manage assets for you when you can't manage them for yourself. "

Jerry and Pat exchanged a knowing smile, appreciating Peggy's obvious enthusiasm for her subject. Peggy definitely relishes the opportunities trusts afford her clients!

Through Your Trust, You Can Control Who Determines Incapacity

"Why," effused Peggy, "a trust can even provide various options for the *determination* of mental disability! There are at least four ways your incapacity could be determined.

"1. The first and simplest option: **You, as the Trustmaker, decide you are no longer comfortable managing your own financial affairs and simply 'resign' as Trustee in favor of your named successor Trustee**! (Okay, so maybe it's not quite as simple as it sounds, since it is indeed a rare individual who recognizes their own mental deficiencies and resigns voluntarily!)

"2. A second option, if you are unable to make this decision independently, is the creation of a '**disability panel.**' The disability panel can be made up of medical experts and family members and friends or a combination of both. The disability panel should have people that know you well and have your best interests at heart, so choosing Cryonics friendly people is essential. When selecting the members of your disability panel, there is a need to consider both the complexity of making the decision versus the protection provided by the people on the panel. You should consider whether having more people on the panel provides a greater sense of protection or creates an unnecessary level of complexity. As the Trustmaker, the choice is yours.

"3. Only if the disability panel is unable to make a determination does the third option arise: **asking the court for its involvement in making a disability determination.** Ideally, your disability panel would make an independent determination of disability (incapacity) without ever having to resort to the court's intervention. In this event, unlike a guardianship, the court's role would be limited to making a determination of incapacity. Your Trustee would still manage your assets.

"4. I should at least mention the last form of disability. This is unlikely, but in the event of an unexplained absence, detention or disappearance, your successor Trustee can take over. I call this **'the Bermuda Triangle'** provision. If the Trustmaker is missing for any reason for a period of at least 30 days, then the successor Trustee can take over the management of the trust assets until the situation is resolved or until there is a legal determination of death.

"Hey," Peggy said, noting Pat and Jerry's skeptical expressions, "as remote as this scenario might seem, it has happened. A quick example before we all take a well deserved break: Years ago, some of our clients took a trip to Greece where their plane crashed and there were no recoverable remains. It took a long time to receive a legal determination of death. In the meantime, the successor Trustee was able to manage the trust assets until a death certificate was received and the process of estate administration could begin.

"Obviously, for cryonicists, the 'Bermuda Triangle' situation could be devastating."

A Simple Solution: The Co-Trustee

"Ultimately, the overarching desire for the cryonicist is to avoid *all* delays in the event of a mental disability. So one possible option to avoid having any type of disability determination is to **appoint a Co-Trustee** to serve during your lifetime. Then, upon disability (or legal pronouncement of death) the Co-Trustee, who is already in an active Trustee role, has no obstacles to acting on your behalf!"

Jerry and Pat looked at each other and said almost simultaneously, "Co-Trustee sounds like the way to go!" With a slightly embarrassed grin, Jerry chuckled, "Yes, Peggy, we have been happily married for so many years we do tend to finish each other's sentences."

General Observations on Trusts as Safeguards Against Guardianship

"The instructions you provide in your Living Trust for the management of your finances and your personal care during mental disability are very important. Many boiler-plate type trusts simply say, 'If two doctors determine the Trustmaker is mentally incapacitated, then the successor Trustee(s) will take over the management of the assets.' Rarely are boilerplate instructions complete as to HOW this day-to-day management is to be accomplished. Trust instructions need to be complete and specific regarding how your assets may be spent on your behalf or on behalf of your loved ones (including pets) if you are no longer directing the actual distribution of assets.

"You should consider crafting instructions that specifically identify the individuals, including yourself, who may benefit from the trust assets during your incapacity. These individuals might include your spouse, your dependent children, other family members who may be dependent upon you for their support, such as parents or siblings, and last but not least, your beloved pets. In addition, you should give good instructions regarding your living conditions, lifestyle, access to friends, family and pets, as well as your specific likes and dislikes regarding your continuing care.

"**And *your* instructions, as cryonicists, should also include specifics regarding your cryonic suspension and related**

special wishes or desires you have. This means including the names and contact information for all persons and organizations critical to your cryopreservation.

"A quick reminder: your successor Trustee or Co-Trustee only has the ability to control the trust assets. Without an agent under a Durable Financial Power of Attorney, your guardian would assume responsibility for assets held outside the trust, like an IRA or annuity. Don't minimize the possibility that things can go wrong at this phase - especially if your IRA, annuity or assets held outside the trust are significant.

"And, of course, remember your instructions must be crafted while you are able and competent, because at some point, for physical or mental reasons, you may not be able to communicate your wishes and desires regarding your care.

"It's so easy to put it off! On more than one occasion, I've encountered individuals in their 80's who are still 'getting around' to making their cryopreservation arrangements and haven't come close to completing their estate planning.

"*Hoping* is not a plan. *Thinking about a plan* is not a plan. *Talking about your plan* is not a plan. Only an *actual completed* plan - where personally crafted legal documents are properly executed and funded - makes the plan work. When it's all said and done, if you don't leave crystal clear instructions, those charged with the responsibility to carry out your wishes won't be provided with guidance for giving you the care you and your loved ones desire and deserve.

"Now, my office dogs are telling me it's time for that little break! Do we all agree?"

Chapter Nine
Your Cryonics Friendly
Durable Financial Power of Attorney

When the threesome returned to their screens, Peggy turned her camera to show her beautiful "office dogs" Abbie and Piper, now happily resting on the floor beside her, staring up at Peggy adoringly.

Pat wiped away a few croissant crumbs. "Looks like the pups are ready for us to all get started again! I gotta say I feel like we are really making progress, Peggy. And you've already given us a pretty good foundation for why the topics coming up are so important."

"That's true, Pat. Each element we tackle supports the other parts of your comprehensive Cryonics Estate Plan. And this Durable Financial Power of Attorney component is critical for everybody, but like the other elements we've talked about, it is especially vital for cryonicists.

"Jerry said you two were familiar with the general idea of the Financial Power of Attorney, but how about if I go over some highlights and as we go along, I'll tie in particular issues for persons who have planned a Cryonics future."

"Sounds good," Jerry responded. "And feel free to assume we know very little. We promise not to get insulted."

What Does a Financial Power of Attorney Do?

"Okay. A Financial Power of Attorney nominates persons or organizations to manage your financial and legal decision-making. The people or organizations you authorize are called your agents (also referred to as your attorneys-in-fact, even though they don't have to be actual attorneys) and they act as a fiduciary with a legal duty to act in your best interest and to preserve your estate plan.

"A Financial Power of Attorney can be drafted so the agent you've nominated has essentially all of the same authority you would have to act on your own behalf. Just think about that for a moment! It's pretty easy to understand why this is potentially such a potent and important instrument!"

Pat looked worried. "Seems like you are really giving away a lot of power."

"True, and that can be either extremely helpful to you at some point or extremely problematic," Peggy answered. "That's why who you nominate to act on your behalf and how the directive defines their authority is so important."

What Powers Can and What Powers Cannot Be Delegated?

"In some states, the delegation of powers can't be done with a broad statement similar to 'you can do anything I can do.' Instead, each power must be specifically delegated. As a result, an artfully drafted Power of Attorney could be 30 or more pages in length! There are powers, sometimes referred to as 'super powers' that need to be specifically delegated, and require your specific consent in the form of initials next to each of the delegated powers.

"And some powers *cannot* be delegated. Essentially, there are five in that category: 1. You can't delegate the power to perform a contract that requires your personal services. For example, if you are a famous artist and you've been hired to paint a mural, that contract is personal to you and cannot be delegated. 2. You can't delegate the right to vote in a public election. 3. You can't delegate a power that someone else has delegated to you. Where this arises is if someone has nominated you as their Trustee and you can't act, then your agent can't take over for you. 4. You can't delegate your ability to sign an affidavit about what you know (because only you know what you know), and 5. you can't delegate the ability to modify or revoke your Last Will and Testament (notice, this does not include the ability to modify, create or revoke a *trust*, a power that *may* be specifically delegated)."

"Hmm, kind of surprising. I never would have thought of what kind of things I could NOT have someone else do for me, but all five of those really do make sense," Jerry commented.

"Even without those five, it sounds like you better have a really trustworthy agent, just like our successor Trustee in our Living Trust!" Pat added. "Can they be the same people you have as your Living Trust Trustees, Peggy?"

The Agent(s) and Their Roles

"Good question. Your Financial Power of Attorney agent(s) may or may not be the same people or organizations you named as your Trustees in your Living Trust, but either way, the job is similar but takes place in a different context. Your agents can only control those assets and activities that are 'outside' of your Living Trust. Typically this might be your life insurance while you are living, your retirement plans, sometimes your house, usually your car and all of the other daily activities that could include the filing of your taxes or the changing of your mailing address, to name a few.

"A Financial Power of Attorney must be carefully drafted to avoid giving too little or too much authority to the agent. In its broadest sense, it will essentially provide the agent with the ability to do everything the principal - that's you - can do, with a few exceptions we've already discussed. You can see why you need to have a detailed conversation with your estate planning attorney regarding this delegation of power and what it might mean for you, for your assets, and, in your case, for your Cryonics goals.

"For cryonicists, a really important aspect of a Durable Financial Power of Attorney is that your agent is not supposed to change your testamentary intent. This means, Pat and Jerry, that if you have a carefully crafted Cryonics Estate Plan (as you soon will have), and if your agent is aware of this plan (you'll make sure of that), they are not supposed to take any action that would disrupt that plan.

"Now, does that mean they *won't* take any such action?" Peggy asked rhetorically. "Uh, not always. It just means that if they do, there would be the right to charge them with a breach of fiduciary duty. The problem here, however, is…Jerry, what would you think?"

Jerry looked thoughtful and ventured, "…That we likely wouldn't even be aware they've made this change? And we won't be in a position to do anything about it?"

"Exactly," Peggy nodded. "So, unless someone else advocates on your behalf, the damage will have been done."

"Can you give us an example of how we could lessen the possibility of our agent going rogue on us?" Pat asked.

"Well, one of my Cryonics clients added specific language that clearly set forth that the agent had no authority to make any changes to his Cryonics-friendly Living Trust and ultimately, his Personal Revival Trust™. He also specified that his agent could not make any changes to the beneficiaries on the life insurance policy that had been specifically purchased for the purpose of funding his cryopreservation and future Revival.

"We can look at some other examples as we put together the language for your Durable Financial Power of Attorney and we'll contemplate the best possible outcomes based on the major decision points."

Factors to Consider

Peggy then led Pat and Jerry through a discussion of major factors to consider when deciding what provisions should be in their Financial Power of Attorney.

Limited vs. General Powers of Attorney

"The first biggee: The primary role of the Financial Power of Attorney is to manage financial assets and make legal decisions. Powers of Attorney can be 'limited' or they can be 'general' in nature. Limited Powers of Attorney list the specific category of acts the agent can perform for the principal, like sell real estate and make tax elections.

"General Powers of Attorney allow the agent to handle essentially *all* financial and legal transactions on behalf of the principal. General Financial Powers of Attorney are preferred because it is not always possible to predict the circumstances under which the Power of Attorney will be required. Boilerplate Powers of Attorney are generally inadequate when it comes to describing those events for which the Power of Attorney will be required."

"What would be some typical actions that would fit under the general powers?" Pat asked.

"Some fairly common ones include the ability to sell or lease a home in the event it becomes necessary to raise funds for your care; the ability to prepare your income taxes; the ability to represent you in a lawsuit for the purpose of bringing the suit or for settling an existing suit; even the ability to make gifts on your behalf for the purpose of long term care asset protection or for estate tax planning purposes, just to name a few. Your average 'off–the-shelf' Power of Attorney does not address all of these concerns. It is recommended you 'plan for the worst and hope for the best, because anything else is just wishful thinking.' And in the legal world, what *can* go wrong, usually does."

"I'm afraid the 'what can go wrong thing' is true in my business as well, and Pat, probably in yours, too?" Jerry wise-cracked. "But those are discussions for another time. So what's our best path forward to proactively solve some of this before it happens, Peggy?"

"Your best defense is to have estate planning directives that contemplate the bizarre and unusual. For the cryonicist, since *much* of this is new territory, this means including provisions in your Powers of Attorney that would be specific to your needs, for example, to make arrangements to transport the cryonicist who has become incapacitated to the location of his Cryonics facility or to make arrangements and sign documents related to the logistics of housing and care near the Cryonics facility."

Durable or Not Durable

"The second biggee: I know it seems counter-intuitive, but unless a Financial Power of Attorney specifically states it is 'durable,' it loses its power when the principal becomes mentally incapacitated."

Pat and Jerry both did a double take and stared at Peggy.

"Yes, you heard me correctly! Only a *Durable* Financial Power of Attorney is useful when planning for mental incapacity."

Pat still looked a little concerned when she said, "Good grief. I hear that guardianship thing raising its ugly head again! So why would anyone *ever* have a NON-Durable Power of Attorney?"

Peggy answered Pat with a smile and a soothing voice. "Well, there are actually some times when that makes sense. An example of a Power of Attorney that might not be 'durable' would be one intended for an immediate or short-term purpose like the transfer of a car title."

"Ok, I can understand that," Pat responded more calmly. "But then, can a 'durable' version last forever?"

"Interesting you asked that. Historically, financial institutions have raised objections to Powers of Attorney that were older than a specific number of years on the grounds they were 'stale.' This, despite state laws that allow the Power of Attorney to exist indefinitely (at least until the legal death of the principal) unless a specific expiration date was stated or the Power of Attorney had been revoked.

"I can see by your faces that you get the irony here. If the Power of Attorney is determined to be 'too old' and the principal must execute a new one, and the principal is now incapacitated, the purpose for which the Durable Financial Power of Attorney was created in the first place has been thwarted. The end result could be the dreaded - yes, Pat, you saw this coming - court-ordered guardianship."

Immediate vs. Springing Powers of Attorney

"On to the third big decision point. Pretty much just what it sounds like: your Power of Attorney can be written so your agent can act immediately. Or (in some states), it can be written so that the directive does not become effective until a particular event occurs, typically your incapacity, at which time the power 'springs' into action.

"Practically speaking, each option has its pros and cons.

"If your agent is authorized to act immediately, they can use the Power of Attorney to act on your behalf as soon as the directive is signed, without hurdles. This can be good news or bad news. The good news is that it works *now*. The bad news is that your agent may use the Power of Attorney in a way that you did not expect and are not so happy with!

"An immediately effective Power of Attorney has the same effect as taking out your checkbook, signing a number of blank checks and handing the checkbook over to your agent! This works great if you have a good and trusting relationship with your agent. It may be a concern, however, if you have to think long and hard to name someone you can trust in this capacity.

"Again, there is good news and bad news associated with a springing Power of Attorney. In states where this is still recognized, the directive does not become effective until a particular event occurs. That event usually is when the principal is no longer capable of making their own financial decisions. The good news is you maintain complete control while you are still capable of making your own decisions.

"The bad news is your agent has to jump through some hurdles to prove that the triggering event has occurred. The agent will need to satisfy financial institutions or individuals to whom the Power of Attorney is presented that you are, in fact, incapacitated. How is this done? Likely the proposed agent will have to present sufficient evidence of the principal's incapacity. Then, that evidence will have to be evaluated by each and every financial institution where the Power of Attorney is presented, resulting in significant delays and potential unexpected results.

"Here is where that good attorney can help their clients maximize the pros and minimize the cons of the options. For example, in some states, like Florida, all Durable Financial Powers of Attorney are immediately effective. As an alternative to a springing Durable Financial Power of Attorney, the directive could be placed in escrow with your estate planning attorney and only released upon the occurrence of certain conditions.

"I know this is a lot to take in. Let me stop for any questions you might have, particularly from your cryonicist's point of view. Jerry, what's on your mind?"

"Well, I've never seen how a Power of Attorney is actually used," Jerry responded. "And with the springing element, I can see some benefits, but how could that work if it takes me being incapacitated to 'spring' my agent's power?"

"Jerry, you've picked up on a powerful potential problem for your Cryonics plans. Here's a play by play of how the approval process to actually use the springing power might go. Your agent goes into your bank and presents the springing Power of Attorney with a written letter from two doctors documenting the mental incapacity of the principal (you - the person who created the Power of Attorney). The bank teller or manager or customer relations manager doesn't have the authority to decide whether this evidence is sufficient. They then require the information provided must be submitted to their legal department for review. The legal department is generally not located on site and many times not even located in the same state. The legal department will then need an attorney who is familiar with your state law so they can make a determination of the validity of the document.

"And this will take, oh, say, what do you think – minutes, hours, days, possibly weeks? It will likely be the latter. As a result, **springing powers of attorney are *not* recommended for Cryonics enthusiasts because they create too many unknown obstacles and could result in delays that would have catastrophic results.**

"Pat, what are you thinking?"

Pat took a few seconds to get her thoughts organized. "Hmm, let me see if I'm getting what you are saying to me as a card-carrying cryonicist: Springing powers of attorney, although they look like they would provide us greater protection because the agent can't act without proof of mental disability, could in actuality be a disaster for us. The unpredictable delays in 'springing that power up' could result in our agent not being able to act in a time of crisis. And Peggy, as you know better than almost anyone, timing for Cryonics is kinda THE big thing. If I'm getting that part straight, Peggy, what other factors do we need to consider as you help us get this Power of Attorney as perfect as possible?"

"Well, first, you are 'spot on' (as my British friend says!) describing the cryonicists' problem with springing powers, and, yes, there are a few more factors I'll want you to consider."

Unlimited vs. Limited Gifting

"The fourth decision point. The self-dealing rules governing agents prohibit them from giving the principal's assets to themselves or to family members without specific authority in the directive to do so. Your Durable Financial Power of Attorney should clearly state the scope of the gifting authority: limited (either a specific amount or a formula) or unlimited. Gifting authority can be an important strategy to reduce taxes or even for long term care asset protection so you likely don't want to leave it out."

Dual Agents vs. Alternate Agents

"Biggee number five. Kind of some nice choices here, but ones that also can cause trouble, since we are all human. You as the principal can nominate one agent. Alternatively, you can nominate two or more agents, with you determining their working relationship. Multiple agents can be authorized to act together; to act independently of each other; or one can be nominated as a 'runner-up' when the initial agent can't serve. Here's the human part: problems can arise when two authorized agents disagree or if third-parties require proof of the first agent's inability to serve, so you'll want to carefully consider your choices."

Pat interrupted, "These are some really big decisions we'll need to be making soon. As we get new information or as our life circumstances change, or if our agent decides to go rogue on us, is there any way to revise or revoke a POA?"

Revoking a Power of Attorney

"Yes, you can revoke a Power of Attorney any time while you are mentally competent. That said, communicating to other people that you have revoked the Power of Attorney can have its challenges. To revoke a Power of Attorney, you need to execute a written revocation and then deliver a copy of the revocation to any financial institutions and third parties (including, of course, your nominated agent) that might have been given the power originally. It might be necessary to record the revocation in the public records for the purpose of 'putting the world' on notice. If you have filed a copy of your POA with your county recorder's office, as some attorneys recommend, you must also record your revocation with *that* office."

Final Thoughts on the Power of the Power of Attorney

"You can check out your *Handbook* Chapter Nine to review what we've just discussed. Everything we've talked about underscores that there are a lot of decisions that go into drafting a Durable Financial Power of Attorney to meet the principal's specific needs. And that goes *double*, once again, for you as cryonicists."

Jerry agreed. "I hear you! I'm astounded by how important our selection of agents becomes for managing our personal business if we are unable to take care of things ourselves!"

"And it seems the persons we select and the powers we give them could potentially make or break our Cryonics dreams," Pat added.

"I appreciate that you two are taking this process so seriously," Peggy responded. **"**You clearly have internalized the critical messages that:

"*Everyone* needs to have a Financial Power of Attorney, readily accessible for those who might need it. In most situations, and *definitely* for cryonicists, the Financial POA should be DURABLE!

"If you fail to create a Durable Financial Power of Attorney while you are mentally competent, the only way someone will be able to make decisions for you would be through the (yes, I think I know what you are about to say)" . . .

"*Dreaded guardianship*!" all three said together in a mock monster voice.

After a joint giggle at their dramatic endeavor, Peggy continued. "Let me add another message we've been dealing with, but maybe I haven't specifically articulated: **When you are evaluating the effectiveness of any advance directive, you will always be balancing the complexity of the requirements with the protections provided by that directive.**

"All of these points will be reiterated again as we continue through the planning process. Next time we'll focus on the Cryonics friendly Healthcare Power of Attorney, HIPAA, and Living Wills, and then we'll have Rudi join us to work on the Objection to Autopsy issues."

"And indeed it will be great to see Rudi again," Jerry kidded, "and in his honor, as he often says when we end a session with him, 'Let's put this meeting in the win column and how about some food?' Okay, I admit, I added the food part. Sorry 'bout that, Rudi."

Chapter Ten
Healthcare Directives and Your Cryonics Friendly Durable Healthcare Power of Attorney

In case you were wondering, Jerry did get his food after the meeting, enjoying an excellent Italian meal. And over the next two weeks, he and Pat debated, (okay, came close to at least two actual serious arguments), discussed, researched, shared, thought about and finally came to consensus on a multitude of estate-related decisions.

With some hard work behind them, a good communications protocol in place, and some tangible directives almost completed, they were feeling very positive when they next met virtually with Peggy.

"Good morning, Pat and Jerry! Ready for this next set?"

"We are primed and ready," Pat enthused.

"But I admit, these next three directives (the Healthcare POA, the HIPAA thing, and the Living Will) have me confused," Jerry jumped in. "It seems like they are so alike, but different, and I can't tell which one is supposed to do what. Pat, in your hospital job I know you deal with this all the time, but, man, it seems convoluted to me!"

"My guess is most people would agree with you, Jerry," Peggy said, "because it IS confusing! Start with the fact that various levels of government are involved. And there is a great deal of overlap in the purpose of these three instruments. *And* there are different ways the same issues are handled in different jurisdictions. *And,* to add to the confusion, different names are used across various jurisdictions for similar sets of circumstances. Frequently used generic terms, for example, include 'healthcare proxy,' or 'healthcare surrogate.'

"It is precisely because of this confusion that we thought it would be most informative—particularly for those jurisdictions that *require* three distinct directives—to discuss each directive separately."

"Sounds reasonable," Jerry responded. "But, Peggy, can you first give us just the ten cent version of what this part is all about?"

What Are Healthcare Directives?

"You bet. Here's the not-so-official dime version: healthcare directives authorize agents or surrogates to make **medical** decisions for you when you are unable to make your own **healthcare related** decisions.

"The directives come into play in two separate circumstances: 1. every day medical care decisions (typically handled by a Durable Healthcare Power of Attorney); and 2. end of life decisions, typically handled by a Living Will." Peggy paused and looked at Jerry for confirmation that her overview had helped him clarify his thinking.

Jerry nodded. "Got it. Thanks. That gives me a framework to wrap around this section. Sounds a whole lot like the Durable Financial Power of Attorney process, except it's for *medical* issues and includes a separate end of life element."

"Exactly, Jerry. Let me stop here and share a few other pieces of general information related to healthcare directives."

Legal Formalities Related to Healthcare Directives

"State laws on healthcare directives, sometimes also referred to as proxies, require they be executed with certain legal formalities. The formalities differ from state to state, but typically healthcare directives need to be signed before a notary and/or before two disinterested witnesses who are present with you when you sign your signature.

"Some people are generally *ineligible* to be witnesses to these directives: anyone who is related to you by blood, marriage, or adoption; your attorney-in-fact (the person you appointed as your agent under a Durable Financial Power of Attorney);

and your doctor or the administrator of the care facility where you are receiving care."

"An interesting set of categories! The commonality being they all might have a financial or emotional vested interest?" Jerry asked. "Actually makes some sense."

"Indeed it does," Peggy agreed.

Where To Keep Your Healthcare Directives

"Oh, and then another important consideration: you need to think about how you and your designated decision maker can organize your directives so they are accessible *where* you need them, *when* you need them.

"I know you understand - especially you, Pat, working at the hospital - that these proxies are only useful if they are available to your agents and healthcare providers in a medical emergency. You'll want to provide a copy to each agent you have named and to your doctors. You should also have one readily available for yourself, particularly when you travel. Copies of the properly executed directives are as good as an original so no need to carry the originals with you.

"If you are traveling frequently, I'd advise you to keep a copy of your healthcare directives on a 'thumb drive' or stored somewhere in the Cloud for easy access. And if you ever reside regularly in more than one state, make sure your directives comply with the standards of your alternate state as well as your home state. Although the full faith and credit principles of the U.S. Constitution *should* permit a directive properly drafted in the home state to be honored in other states, it just makes sense to reduce the chance that a healthcare provider could challenge the legality of your directive based on some technicality.

"Jerry, with your tech background, you may already be aware of a variety of other possible virtual storage options. For a small subscription fee, you can file your directives with a repository company so they can be readily available via fax to healthcare providers worldwide, 24/7. The repository provides a wallet card with instructions on how to obtain the directives when needed; you just keep that card alongside your health insurance cards.

"And - the old fashioned practice that still may be your most direct way to convey your time-sensitive, explicit instructions: your Cryonics organization medical bracelet and/or dog tags. We also recommend you display your critical medical instructions and protocols in a frame next to your desk.

"When you complete your Cryonics Estate Planning with our firm, you'll each have a clearly labeled three ring binder which includes your *full* legal instructions. You'll want to have those binders accessible to be easily grabbed if you ever need to leave the house in a hurry."

"Sounds like important things we actually have to take care of *before* we are in a crisis!" Pat observed.

The Durable Healthcare Power of Attorney and Cryonics

"For sure, Pat. So, with that general background," Peggy went on, "let's start with the Durable Healthcare Power of Attorney. It addresses concerns related to everyday medical care decisions. Situations can occur when you might be unable to speak for yourself but you don't meet the criteria for invoking your Living Will and your end of life decisions (which we'll discuss in a bit.) For instance, you might experience a stroke that temporarily makes you unable to speak or write. In that event, you will need someone to sign medical consent forms and authorize your medical providers regarding your medical care and treatment.

"The purpose of your Durable Healthcare Power of Attorney is to identify the person(s) you trust who are authorized to make most healthcare decisions for you if you lose the capacity to make informed healthcare decisions for yourself."

Jerry gave her a questioning look. "When you say 'most,' what kind of decisions are you talking about?"

"Typically, the types of decisions made with a Durable Healthcare POA are everyday type medical care decisions that would include: consent to surgery; consent to treatment; transfer to or from a medical facility; the hiring and firing of nurses, doctors and therapists; as well as the release of medical information and records.

"Of course, you should always choose someone you believe will make the same type of healthcare related decisions you would make for yourself on these issues."

Pat spoke up. "Deja vu, all over again. Who you pick as your agent is a critical theme of everything we've talked about!"

"So true, Pat. But in addition to *who* that agent is, the *powers* you confer also matter. For example, just like with a Durable Financial Power of Attorney, a Durable Healthcare Power of Attorney might be effective immediately upon signature, or you could make it 'springing,' so it is effective only in the event you are unable to make your own medical care decisions. (By the way, that choice may depend on your state of residence.)

"And, according to how you set it up, you can expand or limit the specific types of healthcare decisions your agent can make for you. For instance, you could authorize your agent to consent to surgical procedures for you but limit their ability to move you to a different healthcare facility. Or you might include specific directions for your agent regarding healthcare decisions that invoke religious beliefs, such as for blood transfusions or for other procedures.

"As cryonicists, you'll want to make sure your agents know how you feel about all those typical processes we mentioned and are thoroughly on board for carrying out your cryonic wishes.

"That's why your Durable Healthcare Power of Attorney is so critical. **Your agent can only carry out your wishes if they know what those wishes are,** so the directions you provide need to be straightforward and organized. And as part of your Cryonics friendly Durable Healthcare POA, you'll want clear written instructions regarding your future cryopreservation, including contact information for your cryopreservation organization, a reference to your contract number, and detailed logistical information related to your standby team. You never know when a seemingly ordinary healthcare event might become a life-threatening crisis!"

Pat and Jerry were silent for a moment, contemplating the significance of Peggy's words. Jerry then spoke for them both. "And what you have reminded us of, Peggy, is that for almost any agent we choose as our healthcare representative, this will be their *first* time to represent cryonicists! We need to help educate them so they can carry out our intentions. With your help, Peggy, we got this! Now why should we care about this HIPAA thing?"

Chapter Eleven
What About the Health Information Portability and Accountability Act and Your Cryonics Plans?

As the group was getting ready to dive into the next topic, the cameras picked up the dogs in both locations. Peggy's dog Abbie seemed to be communicating with Pat and Jerry's two rescue dogs. "I think HIPAA's pretty excited to have so much attention…" may have been the message, although none of the humans speak fluent Dog, so that may not be an exact translation.

What Is HIPAA and Why Is It So Important?

"Pat, you work as a hospital administrator, so I know you are well acquainted with the Health Information Portability and Accountability Act. How about we do a turn-about and you give us *your* ten-cent version of what it is about?"

"Be happy to, Peggy, because, yes, I am keenly aware of its impact every day at work. But since anyone can get reams of detailed history and updated information by just googling 'HIPAA,' how about I give you my nickel version?

"The Health Information Portability and Accountability Act was passed by Congress and signed by President Clinton in 1996 to help modernize the country's healthcare system. It included five different parts that are really important. Title I, for example protects workers' insurance coverage during job changes or loss.

"The 2003 implementation of the privacy and patient rights sections gave us national standards to protect patients as healthcare providers began keeping more and more sensitive data electronically instead of on paper in a file cabinet. You can imagine the opportunities for scams and fraud if coordinated regulations for storing, transferring, and sharing all that private data weren't in place!"

Concluding her mini-lecture, Pat noted: "And, thanks to HIPAA, my CFO can't call up my primary care doctor before our new contract deadline to find out if I have any emerging medical condition that might cost her money! Yes, those things really used to happen!"

"Thanks, Pat, information well worth the nickel! So, among its other roles, HIPAA protects the privacy of your healthcare information and prevents disclosure of that information to unauthorized people. Really important, especially now that so much of our personal information is stored online.

"But, there is another aspect to all this: If you don't take HIPAA regulation seriously, the consequences could run the gamut from minor irritation to major disaster."

Why You Don't Want to Mess With HIPAA

"Jerry, what about you? What's been your experience with HIPAA?" Peggy queried.

"I hadn't thought much about the positive side of this before. I just fill out a form at my clinic each year saying they can share results with Pat. But I've heard stories of family members, even spouses, who couldn't get information on their loved ones because they weren't on a HIPAA list. I assume the stories are true."

"Probably so. I've had some personal HIPAA experiences along those lines," Peggy said, and then shared two stories. Once, while travelling out of town, she had been unable to obtain a copy of her own contact lens prescription because she had failed to designate herself in advance, in writing, at her doctor's office. "It didn't matter that I was giving them verbal authorization over the phone or that I was seeking this information on my own behalf!

"Another story. I got a call one day from one of my clients whose husband was in the hospital in a coma. When she needed to contact the husband's insurance company to discuss his benefits eligibility, the insurance company refused to talk with her because she was not the insured. Her husband was clearly unable to communicate on his own behalf, yet she had not been properly designated as his personal representative under HIPAA, so they could not even talk to her about his situation. Sad, but true."

Implications of the Health Information Portability and Accountability Act for Cryonicists

Peggy continued. "Under HIPAA regulations that became effective in June 2003, you may name a 'personal representative' for the purpose of transacting business on your behalf with your healthcare providers and insurers. Since there is not one nationally-accepted standard HIPAA form for accomplishing that task, your Durable Healthcare Power of Attorney has become especially important as a vehicle to name that personal representative.

"And *critical* for you cryonicists, if one of you is hospitalized, the people at your Cryonics organization need to be able to access detailed health information. Realistically, your healthcare surrogate can't be available 24/7 to provide them what they need.

"**It is therefore *vital* that you sign whatever HIPAA forms are necessary to allow information access to whoever your vendors are** - The Cryonics Institute, Alcor, The American Cryonics Society, Suspended Animation Inc., *whoever* you will be using - so *they* can monitor your condition. Does that all make sense?"

Pat and Jerry were looking thoughtful.

"Are we having fun yet?" Peggy questioned with a smile.

Chapter Twelve
Your Cryonics Friendly Living Will

"Having fun?" Jerry grinned. "Well, I wouldn't go quite that far, but I feel better informed about the positive and potential problematic consequence of HIPAA, even for non-cryonicists! I'm glad you made sure we recognized how important it is for us!"

The cameras picked up the two dogs in California and Peggy's dog, thousands of miles away, seeming to exchange a knowing 'We told you so' vibe.

Living Wills for the General Populace

"And our next topic, the Living Will directive," Peggy stated, "has that same potential to make your lives and those of your loved ones better or more difficult. A Living Will is created to provide written instructions on whether the maker wants life-sustaining treatment or procedures withheld or withdrawn. This would be critical if you can't make informed medical decisions because you are in a terminal or end stage condition, or if you are in a permanently unconscious or persistent vegetative state. Comfort care, such as pain medication, can be continued if it is to reduce pain, even when life-sustaining treatment is not desired.

"The Living Will also permits the maker to specify whether or not they want artificially or technologically supplied food and water. Such treatment may be provided unless there is a specific indication of refusal.

"I'm sure you remember the case of the young woman, Terri Schiavo, who brought Living Wills and life-prolonging procedures into the world view?"

Pat nodded. "Wasn't she in a persistent vegetative state for almost a decade?"

"*Fifteen* years, in fact, Pat, while her husband and her parents fought a legal battle to determine whether she would be removed from life support. That case, coincidentally, took place in Florida (affectionately referred to in some circles as 'God's waiting room') and even the Governor, Jeb Bush, got involved. The lesson from that tragic situation is the importance of making sure your wishes are in writing. Without *written* direction, the medical profession's default position is to keep you alive indefinitely through life-prolonging procedures."

"If I were a doctor," Jerry reflected, "for both ethical and legal reasons, I can certainly understand that as the default position."

"Thus," Peggy paused... "the Living Will.

"A Living Will nominates the people you want to act as your surrogate regarding life-sustaining decisions. The surrogate should not override your instructions and it makes sense to discuss your wishes with potential surrogates to make sure they are aware of your wishes and, in your case, support your Cryonics goals.

"A well-drafted Living Will specifically defines the terms it uses in order to reduce potential dispute over your intended definitions. One example is the use of the phrase, 'persistent vegetative state.' If you want to continue and or to discontinue all forms of life-sustaining treatment, including CPR, you should clearly state your medical preferences in writing.

"If your surrogate is also authorized to execute a Do Not Resuscitate (DNR) order, put that in writing. If you have particular religious or other concerns about the use of blood transfusions or other matters, including a religious objection to autopsy, you should also clearly state your instructions in this and other directives."

"Then a Living Will is not automatically a DNR?" Jerry asked.

"No, a Living Will is NOT a DNR. Sometimes there is confusion. In most states, a DNR can only be obtained with a doctor's consent. The DNR generally states that you do not want cardiopulmonary resuscitation in the event of a heart attack and you do not want resuscitation in the event of a respiratory event. A DNR is printed on a goldenrod-colored piece of paper so it can be easily distinguished from other advance directives. It is often posted above a person's bed, on the refrigerator or on their person.

"And your question, Jerry, provides a good transition into some critical differences between Living Wills for the general populace and Living Wills for cryonicists."

And Living Wills for the Cryonicist: Some Important Distinctions

"For you cryonicists, the Living Will takes on a completely new connotation." Peggy's tone, although calm and professional as always, contained an element of anticipation that made Pat and Jerry sit up straighter and lean in (and made the dogs look up from where they each had been resting). It was clear that what Peggy was about to share was significant.

 "A Living Will may be drafted in a way to take on the characteristics of a *'Will to Live,'* at least until a determination is made that legal death is imminent and your suspension team is in place for the purpose of ensuring an ideal cryopreservation."

Peggy had become very deliberate, slowing her words down to emphasize the gravity of the issue. The dogs relaxed, but Pat and Jerry maintained their deep focus.

"In many ways it is a hybrid type of instruction. Essentially it says, 'Keep me alive long enough for the suspension team to arrive, then stop life-prolonging procedures so I get the best opportunity at a successful cryopreservation.' Some cryonicists may want to specifically indicate a request for hydration, cooling, or other procedures that would improve the chances for the best possible outcomes at suspension time.

"The Living Will, or in your case shall we say the Will to Live, should also be crafted to include all of the important contact information for your suspension team, your preservation organization, and any other persons who should be contacted or made aware of your imminent legal death. Only with very specific and well thought out legal directions can you optimize your prospects for an ideal suspension."

Pat jumped in. "You really have me thinking, Peggy! A Will to Live! This is provocative information."

"AND," Peggy concluded, "a DNR would not be a good choice for the cryonicist unless death was imminent and there was a suspension team standing by.

"Now, since we are getting really good at making sense of topics where cryonicists have distinct needs different from the general populace, let's move into the autopsy issue. Why don't you take a quick break while I bring Rudi into the discussion?"

Chapter Thirteen
Avoiding Autopsy Is Imperative for Cryonicists!

Rudi joined the Zoom group, and after exchanging happy greetings and a bit of mutual catching up on kids, canines, and careers, Peggy steered the meeting back to the topic at hand. "I've asked Rudi to join us because he has been following the issue of autopsies related to Cryonics for a long time and can share some recent sad events as well as some encouraging developments."

Sharing Bad News

"So glad to be with you, and yes, I do have both some disturbing news and then some really good news to share," Rudi began. "I think that pretty much anyone who knows me knows I am hugely optimistic about life and the future (the reason, by the way, I am such a proponent of Cryonics!), but a recent situation has had a negative, visceral impact on me.

"Well, actually not just on me, but on the international Cryonics community. We were recently shocked to learn that one of our own leaders and activists had been autopsied by a coroner in California!

"The reason for the autopsy was that this individual had died an 'unattended death.' Despite the fact that Cryonics technicians were on site promptly and were doing everything they could do to stop the autopsy, it still took place.

"Alcor leadership was so distressed that the Alcor CEO sent out a special video pleading with its membership to take action to minimize the risk of autopsy.

"The video included a request for donations to help fund legal research into the fifty states regarding autopsy statutes and policies. The video also included disturbing images of the actual brain of the Alcor member, now sliced into twenty pieces. Seeing this high-definition documentation of the segmented brain of a long term Cryonics activist, someone who had been in high level leadership at Alcor, was deeply disturbing.

"Pat and Jerry, I know you have done enough research into the processes involved in Cryonics procedures to understand the significance of the problem. The major focus of Cryonics is on preserving the physical structure of the brain so that scientists and medical personnel in the future have the best possible chance of reanimating a member's memories and personal identity. How sad to see that this chance probably is lost for that member!"

Sharing Encouraging News

"Wow, how discouraging that an autopsy could happen even to a professional in the field of Cryonics! So, Rudi, the good news is…?" Jerry asked.

"Happily, several pieces of good news, Jerry. Start with the fact that coroners and medical professionals are increasingly respecting the advance directives of those who wish to avoid autopsy, especially if it is on religious grounds. As Californians, you'll be glad to know that your state has a process where you can prevent autopsy of your remains in most circumstances by signing a certificate stating that autopsy is contrary to your religious beliefs. And that process has already been successful in preventing autopsies.

"Add to that, a growing number of states now have specific statutes restricting the circumstances under which the state can mandate autopsies, giving more freedom to the coroner or medical examiner in your jurisdiction to forego an autopsy.

"And the best news, you two have probably the premier attorney in the world for this particular situation! She will help you do everything legally possible to ensure you avoid autopsy. Peggy, back to you."

Reducing Your Risk of Autopsy

"Thanks for the nice words, Rudi, and I graciously accept the kudos, because our firm really has given this issue serious attention on behalf of our Cryonics clients.

"Pat and Jerry, as part of your Cryonics Estate Plan," Peggy continued, "we will include directives that expressly state you are NOT to be autopsied. At this point in time, we do this by stating that autopsies are against your religion."

Jerry cringed. "Honestly, a number of cryonicists I know personally, frankly including me, are pretty skeptical about the claims of most religions. So using that as the reason to avoid autopsy seems a bit disingenuous, maybe even questionable, to me."

"I appreciate your candor and your ethics," Peggy responded. "And let me clarify: you won't be asked to name a particular religion and you don't need to state what your religion is. But in order to expedite your desire to avoid autopsy, utilizing the language of existing statutes is currently the most practical legal way to protect you from that process."

"I guess that makes sense. Creating more Cryonics friendly laws is a different and longer-term conversation!' Jerry acquiesced.

"Does this directive definitely protect us from autopsies? Oh, and could the person we specify as our Medical POA have the authority to prevent an autopsy?" asked Pat.

"Well, the answer to both questions is 'yes, under most circumstances,'" Peggy responded. "In some very reasonable situations, the rights of the larger society need to take precedence over our individual wishes. Recall that autopsies are typically mandated by law to guard human life, for example, where there is evidence of homicide, suicide, unexplainable accident, or a contagious disease or some unknown cause that could affect others."

Pat nodded her understanding. "It seems like autopsy is another of those critical timing issues. How would the police or a medical examiner know that I don't want to be autopsied, assuming I am declared legally dead in one of those 'not-so-charming' situations you just mentioned where it's mandated?"

"Can I take this question, Peggy?" Rudi jumped in, lifting his wrist up to his camera. "Here's my bracelet that clearly states my objection to autopsy, and in the event my wrist wasn't in too good of shape, I also have all my information on my 'dog tag' neck chain. And, of course, I carry a card in my wallet right next to my driver's license. Oh, *and* my Healthcare surrogates were specifically selected because they support my Cryonics goals and are committed to helping me avoid autopsy. The Cryonics organizations offer these bracelets upon signup."

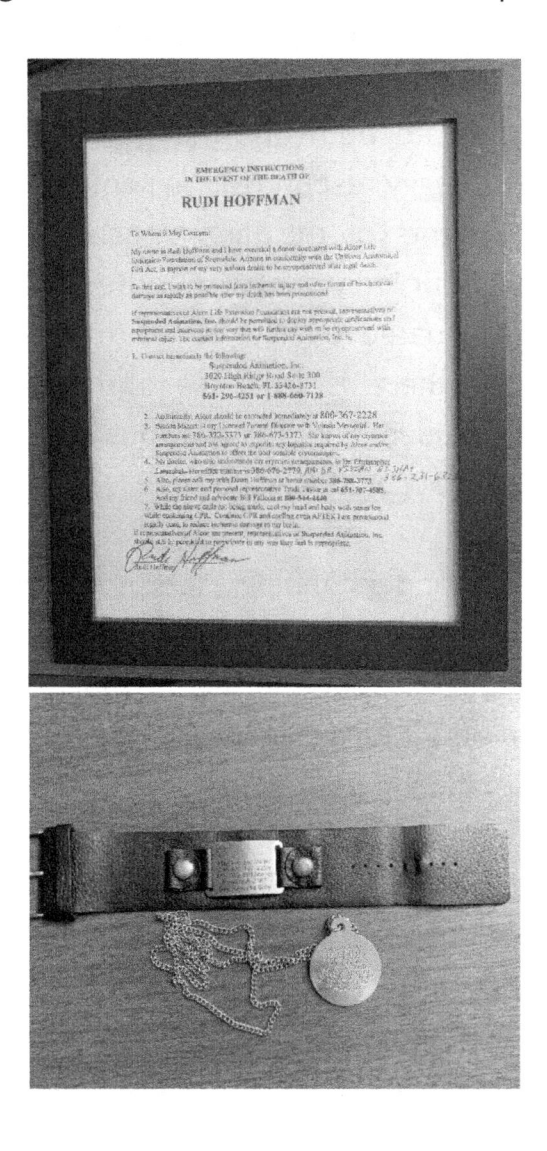

Peggy added, "And this is again where having your critical information in a virtual repository, freely available to caregivers 24/7, would be wise.

"Any other questions for now on avoiding autopsies?" Peggy paused, giving Pat and Jerry time to raise their eyebrows questioningly at each other before looking back at her with a 'We're good, let's move on' nod. "Then let's start to wrap this process up. We'll go over a few more important points, review some critical issues, and answer any final questions you have."

"It's getting exciting and all coming together," Jerry noted. "Rudi, can you stay with us for a bit, since none of the things we'll talk about now are private and some of our final pieces may relate to how the Cryonics and the legal directives mesh? Oh, Peggy, is that okay with you?"

"Of course, if Pat is good with that plan?" Peggy looked at Pat, who gave a very positive thumbs up.

Chapter Fourteen
Additional Considerations for Your Cryonics Estate Plan

The group took a brief break to let their respective dogs out. Yes, there were now SIX beautifully behaved dogs, two at each location, as part of the group! Peggy's dog Abbie was sharing the canine office responsibilities that day with Prince Piper the Pomeranian. Along with Rudi's two peekapoos (Harry Potter and McGonagall) and Pat and Jerry's rescue dogs (Daisy and Buttercup), the six ignored the human conversation and enjoyed a distanced Tail Wag Appreciation Moment (TWAM) as the human group reconvened in front of their computers.

Peggy took the lead. "We've explored Revocable Trusts with your Personal Revival Trust™ provisions and examined how we will handle the Last Will and Testament component, as well as each of the critical healthcare and disability directives. We are happily close to completing this planning portion of our process together, but there are a few additional relevant aspects I want to mention before we get your feedback, questions, and concerns."

Estate Taxes Considerations

"Jerry and Pat, when we first met, you shared with me that you were definitely not in the top 1% of American families financially that need to be seriously concerned about estate taxes. We currently live in a time when the federal estate tax exemption exceeds $11 million per person, $23 million plus for you as a married couple. This 'double' exemption exists because now a surviving spouse can 'claim' the unused exemption of a deceased spouse, sometimes referred to as 'portability.' This was not true in the past.

"Keep in mind that some states still have an estate tax and the exemption amounts for each state can vary. So, depending on where you live at the time of your death, there may be other estate tax concerns at that time.

"If the current estate tax exemption numbers don't sunset or change and return to much lower levels, then not just *your* family, but *most* Americans will never have to worry about or pay an estate tax. I just bring it up because those numbers *can* change by law or *your* circumstances could change; times are clearly unpredictable right now! We'll make sure it is a subject we continue to monitor and it is good motivation to keep your plan reviewed and updated over time.

"If the combined value of your gross taxable estate (basically the total of your worldwide assets) ever exceeds the estate tax exemption, then there are time-tested strategies available for reducing or even eliminating estate taxes. One popular estate tax minimization technique for cryonicists is a testamentary charitable lead trust designed to zero out any estate tax liability that might be due. This strategy contemplates that a stream of income would be paid to a charity or charities of your choice for a sufficiently long period of time to eliminate any estate tax liability that would be due at your legal death. And, since you'll be in cryopreservation, you won't miss the money anyway. This will allow you to support those organizations that might be able to speed up the process of Revival. I'm happy to discuss this and other estate tax planning options further if you like."

Long Term Care Considerations

"That said, a subject we would be remiss if we didn't also mention is long term care. Despite our protests of 'I'm never going to need a nursing home,' there just aren't any guarantees and pretty much every person in a long-term care facility thought *they* would never be there.

 "Pat, as a hospital administrator, you know better than almost anyone how costs of care are rising. The best defense may be a form of insurance, possibly traditional long term care insurance where you pay a premium in exchange for a payment at some daily rate that can be applied to your in-home, nursing home, or assisted living care. But, Rudi, what other types of insurance options might they find?"

"Friends, let me tell you, I am so PROUD to be an insurance and investments professional in this day and age! Years ago, there were so few options, and most were limited in what they offered the client," Rudi beamed. "But with some of the new variations of life insurance I can present to you, you will have a choice of products that combine the best of annuities and life insurance with long term care benefits.

"Get this, if you never need to use the benefits, you can still have the option to 'take it with you.' When we have our follow-up Personal Revival Trust™ funding meeting, Pat and Jerry, we will see what program works best for your family and your Cryonics plans. The simple explanation of this is that modern life insurance policies can enable access to the full death benefit while you are alive if you are terminal or disabled. It really is a great time to be alive! We have SO many better choices for protecting our futures!"

Pat was clearly surprised. "There might be a product that can serve as life insurance to fund our Trust but also could assist with long term care if needed? I am *definitely* looking forward to checking that out with you, Rudi!"

Peggy smiled at Rudi's exuberance and remarked, "Shall we agree for now that as part of your Cryonics Estate Plan we will regularly review and evaluate your potential need for funding long term care?

"And now, what's on your minds?"

Yes, Bad Things Can Happen, But We Can Deal With Them!

Jerry answered for the couple. "Maybe it's because of our volatile professions in high tech and in healthcare administration, but ever since we started the process of becoming cryonicists with a solid estate plan, Pat and I have made kind of a game of thinking about 'What are the worst things that could happen? What haven't we thought of?' So, Peggy and Rudi, what are the worst things that could happen? What haven't we thought of?"

"Hmm, that's actually an exciting question!" Peggy began. "So much of what we are doing has never been tried before. We are all navigating uncharted territory at a time of unprecedented change in legal and scientific frontiers. Let me think about my answer for a minute. Rudi?"

Rudi had clearly worried over this question before, because his answer was direct and immediate. "For me, the worst things that could happen all relate to not being part of potentially the most exciting endeavor in human history, transcending time, transcending even our currently limited bodies."

Peggy jumped back in. "Before we get too philosophical, however, let me share some pragmatic things you'll want to consider to prevent any 'worst case' scenario."

Dying Without a Cryonics Estate Plan

"Dying without a Last Will or Living Trust could be disastrous for cryonicists because the default is that all assets would likely be distributed to the decedent's 'heirs at law'. Assets would not be preserved for the benefit of the revived cryonicist in the future. You two will soon have a full Cryonics Estate Plan in place, so don't need to worry about that 'worst case!' "

Challenges by Disgruntled Family Members

"Some version of the 'disgruntled family members' issue, of course," Peggy continued, "can happen even to non-cryonicists. Unfortunately, some family members who don't support your vision may see it as 'their right' to grab the assets held by your estate, assets that are intended to be available to the revived you. Avoiding this possible problem, of course, is why we are so serious about preparing your Cryonics Estate Plan!"

Rudi interjected enthusiastically, "And this is yet *another* reason why life insurance makes sense to help fund your Cryonics Estate Plan. The proceeds are paid directly to that named beneficiary, whether that be heirs, a Personal Revival

Trust™, or both. Where the money goes is simply irrefutable, at least 99% of the time!"

Lack of an Immediate or an Identifiable Future Beneficiary

Peggy agreed and continued. "Although some legal practitioners may be comfortable with a trust that makes no distributions during the cryopreservation of the Trustmaker, there can be risks in that strategy. It is possible a determination could be made that without an immediate and identifiable beneficiary, the Personal Revival Trust™ fails, and therefore must be distributed.

"Best practice, therefore, would dictate there should be some distribution from the trust while the Trustmaker is in cryopreservation. The logical beneficiary would be the organization that maintains the Trustmaker or other scientific organizations dedicated to researching technologies for life extension and/or future revival. We would not want a court to take the position that since the revival of the cryopreserved Trustmaker is not a certainty, that the trust fails for lack of an identifiable beneficiary. If this determination were made, the trust might be distributed to the 'final beneficiary' as we talked about previously."

The Need for Contingent Final Beneficiaries

"Cryonicists are very optimistic people." Pat, Jerry, and Rudi smiled into their cameras and nodded at Peggy's statement.

"If they can't live forever, then being cryopreserved is the next best thing to a permanent and final death. And, as we are all aware," Peggy added, "we currently do not have the technology to revive a cryopreserved human being and return them to full bodily function with all prior memories intact.

"We can imagine instances that might preclude revival, such as a natural disaster or a catastrophic event that destroys the dewar where the Trustmaker resides. For that reason, your Cryonics Estate Plan will need to be explicit about contingent final beneficiaries in the event the possibility of revival no longer exists."

More Than One Revived "John Doe" Making a Claim on the Trust Assets

Pat spoke up, "Since we are contemplating revival in an unspecified future time (which, given the accelerating rate of change, I bet will be sooner rather than later), I can imagine lots of scenarios that we would previously have thought of as only science fiction. The impact of cloning, for example?"

Peggy responded, "That is not as far out as you think, Pat! Cryonicists surely *may* need to consider the possibility that more than one 'revived Trustmaker' could make a claim on their Personal Revival Trust™ assets. In addition to the actual revived person, there could be a clone of that person! Or perhaps even a cyber-rev entity who has all of the

Trustmaker's memories but none of the other characteristics of the original person."

Jerry did a cigar/eyebrow Groucho Marx imitation and declared,"Ooh, as a tech guy, I think I like that cyber-rev possibility. I've been keeping up with Martine Rothblatt's incredible research. She has now made it possible to download one's personality for free at cyber-rev.org!"

After a pause, Jerry added, "Okay, Peggy and Rudi, so far you haven't come up with any worst case situations that we couldn't have anticipated. Is that the best of the worst you've got?"

Peggy retorted, "Ah, we are all creative people who could dream up all kinds of intriguing negative and positive possibilities for the future, Jerry, but seriously? Ethically, and as professionals, Rudi and I are committed to never promising more than we can deliver. We want you to be fully on board with the risks as well as the potential benefits of the future you are engaging."

The Rule Against Perpetuities, Part 2

Peggy added, "Oh, I know what else needs to be in a list of worst cases. We've talked about it before, but it could mess things up, so I'll bring it up again: the rule against perpetuities (RAP), the idea that a trust cannot have an unlimited life and has to end at some point in the future. I know we've noted that many states have now abolished or extended the rule against perpetuities, theoretically allowing the creation of a trust that can last forever or at least for a substantial period of time. Florida law, for example you remember, allows the estate plan drafter to select a RAP of 360 years, meaning the trust can remain intact until 360 years have elapsed. Then the trust must be dissolved and the assets distributed.

"How can we deal with that problem? Obviously, if there is a point in time when the trust assets have to be distributed and the cryonicist is still in cryopreservation, there must be a 'final beneficiary.' The final beneficiary should, in the context of Cryonics planning, be a charitable organization or its successor. There would likely be no valid way to name an individual who would be alive at the relevant time.

"So many interesting possibilities! And as we complete your Cryonics Estate Plan, you can bet we will anticipate, eliminate, or attenuate as many worst case situations as possible! And now, just a few more pieces of final advice for your consideration..."

Cryonics Friendly Advisors and the Importance of a Team Approach

"Ultimately, Cryonics Estate Planning is not just about legal directives - it's about results," Peggy stated emphatically. "The key is clear, comprehensive, customized instructions for your lifetime care and for your personal and financial preservation in the future.

"You don't want or need a one-size fits all approach to estate and financial planning. The Cryonics Estate Planning arena is one that is so unique that only advisors who have specialized expertise should even venture into this forest of possible lions, tigers and bears (oh my!).

"Estate planning decisions straddle legal, financial, and other advisor categories, so you'll want to ensure that any advisors you work with are comfortable both working collaboratively and with your Cryonics plans.

"Sometimes advisors give conflicting advice, not because the advice is necessarily wrong, but because there can be several ways to achieve a planning goal and advisors look at the goal from their own planning perspective, a form of planner 'tunnel vision'. Tunnel vision, however, can cause unintended consequences.

"An example might occur when a non-legal advisor recommends that a parent add an adult child's name to the parent's bank account as a strategy to avoid probate. The parent, child and non-legal advisor might not fully understand that the joint account is now subject to the child's creditors if the child faces a divorce or lawsuit. Under the circumstances, the parent might select a different method to avoid probate."

"Really good - and again thought-provoking - advice, Peggy!" Pat noted.

"Thank you, Pat, this is not our first rodeo. Our firm has a three part process we recommend as you proceed with your Cryonics Estate Plan.

The short version:

Part 1. Work with counseling-oriented advisors (attorneys, insurance and financial advisors, tax professionals and others) who teach you the questions you didn't even know you needed to ask.

Part 2. Develop a system that includes education, updating, and maintenance of your Cryonics Estate Plan, and

Part 3. Create long-term professional relationships with Cryonics friendly advisors who will work together and with your loved ones to insure your Cryonics goals are achieved.

"Just one more area I need to emphasize before we turn this over to Rudi to help us transform this planning process into action."

Ethical Considerations

"All of your advisors, but particularly attorneys, must address their ethical duties to their client, either as an individual or as a couple. When an attorney represents a couple, issues can sometimes arise if the couple is not aligned on the overall estate planning objectives.

"The rules that govern attorneys require them to zealously represent the interests of their client. If an attorney represents more than one client on the same matter, conflicts of interests can present themselves. If the conflict between the parties cannot be resolved, then the attorney is prevented from representing both parties and new counsel will be required. Pat and Jerry, if at any time you feel that you and your partner will not have common estate planning goals - especially around the topic of Cryonics - then you would be advised to have separate legal counsel.

"Creating an estate plan that works requires commitment. It also requires an acknowledgement that the plan you create today may not be the plan you need (or want) in the future. Life is dynamic, your estate plan should be, too. This has never been more true than in the current social and economic climate where the only thing that is certain is CHANGE.

"Pat and Jerry, I hope you now feel like you have enough information to make some really important decisions for your personal and financial future. Learning about new techniques and assimilating a new language for legal concepts and directives can be overwhelming. But, like the old adage, 'Sometimes the only way to eat an elephant is one bite at a time.' Rudi and I both appreciate all the time, energy and effort you've committed to this process, to your family and to your future."

Chapter Fifteen
Moving Towards Immortality: Four Simple Action Steps

When the foursome reconvened a few weeks later, the humans (and their canines) exchanged greetings and the mood was jubilant. "Pat and Jerry," Rudi began, "Peggy and I want to reach across the five thousand kilometers that separate Florida and California and extend congratulations to you both. This has been a long journey, but you have had the vision and perseverance to see it through.

"And I have great news for you about your policies. They have both been approved as applied!"

Jerry and Pat got up from their seats to do a little dance and hug each other. Looking satisfied, Jerry exclaimed, "What I think that means is - that in addition to the policies we have to solidly fund our Cryonics plans - we now have these policies that fund our Cryonics Estate Plan with the beautiful leverage of life insurance. Did I get that right?"

"You are absolutely right, Jerry!"

Jerry further observed, "You know, Rudi, what really made a difference is how you worked with us to incorporate this into our budget. ***AND*** **the fact that we have these policies not just as funding for our Personal Revival Trust™, but also as tax-free retirement savings,** ***AND*** **as long-term-care insurance. These policies are doing triple duty!"**

Rudi graciously acknowledged the compliment. "Well, we have been able to work well together, and it has been great fun! Because you folks were willing to candidly share your financial and family situation, it was easy for Peggy and me to understand your values, resources, and circumstances.

"And look what you two have accomplished! Let me screen share **Appendix C** from the *Handbook,* the four steps for completing your Cryonics Estate Plan, and I'm thinking we can check them all off!"

Appendix C appeared on their screens:

Appendix C
Four Steps for Completing Your Cryonics Estate Plan

- ❑ **1.** Contact Rudi to **Sign with a Cryonics Organization** if you are not yet a Cryonics member. See **Appendix B** and contact Rudi at RudiHoffman.com or 386-235-7834.

❏ **2.** Contact Rudi to **Fund Your Preservation and Your Financial Future,** to help you be "Affordable as well as Immortal." RudiHoffman.com; 386-235-7834.

❏ **3.** Contact Peggy to **Create Your Cryonics Estate Plan,** including your Personal Revival Trust™. Peggy@HoytBryan.com; 407-977-8080.

❏ **4.** Work with Peggy to **Commit to a Process to Maintain Your Estate Plan.**

Peggy jumped in to add her congratulations. "Yep! You two can check off all four boxes! You've signed with a Cryonics organization, funded your project through Rudi, completed your Cryonics Estate Plan and developed a process to maintain that plan with me!

"And, Pat and Jerry," Peggy continued, "I'm so pleased that **you have your Personal Revival Trust™ set up and you have worked with your financial organizations and advisors to re-title your assets and update your beneficiary designations so that your Trust is properly funded.** Really well done!"

Back on the group screen, Rudi smiled. "I know you two have been following along in the *Handbook* as you've worked on this process. You now have accomplished everything listed in the *Handbook*'s **Appendices B and C**!

"So, friends, let's stop for a moment to take a deep breath and to zoom out from the details to focus on the bigger picture here. What we have achieved as a team is pioneering, historic, and even epic! A few well educated, visionary humans (if we may say so ourselves!) working together in the twenty-first century have crafted credible plans to be alive and truly *thriving* maybe even hundreds of years from now!

"And the reason we are doing this is that your lives are important! Could you just take a moment to tell us what you value most about your lives and why you are committed to extending them? Pat and Jerry, why are your lives irreplaceable and special? What contributions, experiences, and adventures do you want in your future?"

Dear Reader,
At this point in the book, we are going to leave Pat and Jerry thinking about their answers . . . and ask YOU to respond to these life-affirming questions. How would you answer for YOUR life?

While we have used our composite, fictional, but reality-based characters to make this book more readable, executing your Cryonics goals and Cryonics Estate Planning is *not* about Pat and Jerry Reynolds. It is first and foremost about YOU, and whatever it is that is most precious to you about your life. What we are after here is a deep connection to the part of you that we are trying to save and preserve for the future.

Take a minute and look around the room where you are reading this. Intentionally step back from the mundane and realize how remarkable it is that the Universe has arranged trillions of molecules to create the unique consciousness that is *you*. It has taken literally billions of years to configure the atoms that make up the human who just completed this sentence. While we are still expanding our understanding of the intricate processes of adaptation, somehow matter has evolved and learned to contemplate itself. Understand itself. Consider its own transience. And even take action to overcome the all-too-soon dissolving of that consciousness caused by entropy and death.

Kings and queens, tyrants and saints, sages and poets, mystics and scientists, every wise and profound human who has ever lived (and is now irretrievably dead) . . . none have had the opportunity to do what you can do today. It is the unique set of converging systems that allow us to leverage technology and finance to accomplish goals like overcoming senescence and death that were never before close to being feasible.

The Pharaohs, with all their power over thousands of subjects, seem to have spent their lifetimes trying to prepare for an afterlife of abundance. But even those wealthy privileged rulers could not do what we can do. . . what you have the power to do if you will but act now. These earlier humans simply did not have the tools or the foundational underpinnings of the Enlightenment to make their plans for an afterlife realistically possible.

The brilliant stoics of Greece have endowed us with writings that reveal a depth and understanding of human nature with such clarity that they seem to have been penned last week, not several millennia ago. These seminal thinkers put an emphasis on taking action on that which was amenable to change, while accepting with equanimity and grace those situations which no amount of effort or creativity could change. Primary among those things which even the prodigious wisdom of a Marcus Aurelius or Epictetus acknowledged as intractable was the inevitability of death.

"Brief is man's life and small the nook of the Earth where he lives; brief, too, is the longest posthumous fame, buoyed only by a succession of poor human beings who will very soon die and who know little of themselves, much less of someone who died long ago."
~ Marcus Aurelius

"I cannot escape death, but at least I can escape the fear of it."
~ Epictetus

And, in their time, these words were undeniably correct.

There are perhaps no words to adequately convey the unique moment we have been given in the history of the Universe. Our ancestors were much like us; some were no doubt much more intelligent than you or me. However, they had superstitions to overcome their evanescence. We have Science.

Practice of that Science has already provided substantive "proof of concept" validation of the principles underlying cryonics.

We have no idea why we have been given this opportunity, and those possibly more deserving who came before us have not. We'll add this to the obvious lack of fairness in the way reality seems to be structured. But please, members of our human family, do not take this gift of timing you have been granted and neglect to do your part. Many pages ago, we started with a quote from John Adams we will close with, "We can not guarantee success, but we can deserve it."

We are not going to let Pat and Jerry answer the questions about what makes life worthwhile. Because we want YOU to focus on *your* answers to "Why should you do everything you can to continue to be alive?" And the related question, "Are you ready to take some actions that may let your aliveness continue and flourish?" If we authors have done our job, you now understand that Cryonics Estate Planning is REAL. And you now are looking forward to establishing the best Cryonics Estate Plan possible.

Let's review the four big themes we hope you appreciate after reading this book.

Four Takeaways

1. Cryonics is a legitimate, though currently unproven, medical intervention. Assuming cryonics does indeed work and you are revived, it will probably be in a really spectacular and intriguing future.

2. Cryonicists will want to have resources to fund their resuscitation and to provide options for their future life through careful Cryonics Estate Planning.

3. Cryonics and Cryonics Estate Planning may well be affordable for you through the leverage of life insurance and specifically designed annuities.

4. There are resources and people to help you in your research and decision-making. Peggy and Rudi are two of those helpful and accessible resources!

And literally right this moment, you can take steps to make your vision reality. Appendices B and C spell out the details.

We have come to the conclusion of our journey together *for now*. From our awareness of pushing keyboard buttons here in Florida to the consciousness magically decoding the resulting symbols wherever you are located, may we extend our deepest respect and admiration. And even recognition. Because, at some level, your deepest self and our deepest selves may be truly parts of the same Universal Whole.

We have compelling evidence to document that the arc of human progress is positive and will continue to be so. The possibilities available to you in that future will grow exponentially, likely in ways we can't even imagine at this point. You are a significant part of this long-range arc of human progress! To our FUTURE!

We look forward to hearing from you.

Rudi Hoffman, Port Orange, FL
Peggy Hoyt, Oviedo, FL
Nov. 2, 2020, CE

Appendices

These items did not fit seamlessly into the book narrative but contain information that serious cryonicists can appreciate.

- **Appendix A: Four Takeaways From the Book**

- **Appendix B: Ten Steps to Take If You Have <u>NOT</u> Yet Signed Up for Cryonics**

- **Appendix C: Four Steps for Completing Your Cryonics Estate Plan**

- **Appendix D: Cryonics Planning: The Cryonics Decision Tree™**

- **Appendix E: Table of Consanguinity**

- **Appendix F: 7th Annual Dynasty Trust State Rankings Chart**

Appendix A
Four Takeaways From the Book

Here are the four big themes we hope were obvious in the book.

Four Takeaways From the Book

1. Cryonics is a legitimate, though currently unproven, medical intervention. Assuming Cryonics does indeed work and you are revived, it will probably be in a really spectacular and intriguing future.

2. Cryonicists will want to have resources to fund their resuscitation and to provide options for their future life through careful Cryonics Estate Planning.

3. Cryonics and Cryonics Estate Planning may well be affordable for you through the leverage of life insurance and specifically designed annuities.

4. There are resources and people to help you in your research and decision making. Peggy and Rudi are two of those helpful and accessible resources!

Appendix B
Ten Steps to Take if You Have <u>NOT</u> Yet Signed Up for Cryonics

(If you ARE already signed up, please proceed to Appendix C.)

- ❏ 1. Go to **RudiHoffman.com** and fill out the "Quote Request" form.
- ❏ 2. Set a phone/skype video visit appointment on the web-based calendar.
- ❏ 3. View the four short videos under the "Cryonics" tab of the website.
- ❏ 4. Discuss options with Rudi Hoffman; make informed decisions on Cryonics vendor, amount and type of life insurance preferred.
- ❏ 5. Sign the pre-completed application sent to you; mail or scan/email this back to Rudi.

- ❏ 6. Complete the local nurse exam and separate health history phone call.
- ❏ 7. About 6 weeks of underwriting later, you receive your policy. Return any needed requirements to put policy in place.
- ❏ 8. Contact Cryonics organization and complete their application. (Rudi will have sent them a full copy of your policy.)
- ❏ 9. Receive your Cryonics bracelet and/or neck chain.
- ❏ 10. *Congratulations, you deserve to celebrate. You are a fully signed and funded cryonicist!*

CHECK OFF 1-10? PLEASE PROCEED TO APPENDIX C, Four Steps for Completing Your Cryonics Estate Plan

Appendix C
Four Steps for Completing Your Cryonics Estate Plan

❏ **1.** Contact Rudi to **Sign with a Cryonics Organization** if you are not yet a Cryonics member. See **Appendix B** and contact Rudi at RudiHoffman.com or 386-235-7834.

❏ **2.** Contact Rudi to **Fund Your Preservation and Your Financial Future,** to help you be "Affordable as well as Immortal." RudiHoffman.com; 386-235-7834.

❏ **3.** Contact Peggy to **Create Your Cryonics Estate Plan,** including your Personal Revival Trust™. Peggy@HoytBryan.com; 407-977-8080.

❏ **4.** Work with Peggy to **Commit to a Process to Maintain Your Estate Plan.**

Appendix D
Cryonics Planning: The Cryonics Decision Tree™

Your Cryonics Estate Plan will include a Revocable Living Trust with resulting Personal Revival Trust™ as your primary planning instrument. It will be supplemented by a Pour-Over Last Will, Durable Financial Power of Attorney, Healthcare Power of Attorney with Cryonics Provisions, Cryonics Friendly Living Will, Religious Objection to Autopsy, and Pre-Need Guardian Declaration. All directives are created under the laws of the State of Florida. If necessary, we will be happy to coordinate with out of state legal co-counsel of your choosing at no additional charge. Legal fees for out of state counsel are not included in our quoted fees.

Below are some helpful questions for you to think about prior to beginning the Cryonics Estate Planning process.

Alive and Well:
1. Will you serve as the initial Trustee of your Trust? Likely the answer to this question is yes. Will there be a co-trustee?
2. If you don't plan to serve as initial Trustee, will your initial Trustee be a person or a corporate Trustee? Who?

3. What assets will your Trust own during your lifetime? Do you own any cryptocurrencies or other digital assets? Any unusual assets? Remember, your trust only controls those assets that it owns or that ultimately name the trust as the beneficiary. Jointly held assets or assets that name an individual beneficiary will not be controlled by your trust or your Last Will. Individually owned assets (not retirement plans) should be re-titled to the name of your Trust.
4. What assets do you have with beneficiary designations? Example, life insurance policies, retirement plans and annuities. Please provide copies of account statements for all assets along with change of beneficiary forms. All beneficiary designations should be updated to reflect your Trust as a named beneficiary.
5. Do you own any real estate? Please provide copies of all deeds. You may want to transfer the ownership of your real property to your Trust.
6. Do you own any business interests? Please provide copies of entity formation or corporate documents. Are these interests controlled by a Buy-Sell Agreement? Do you want to assign your business interests to your Trust?
7. Who will be your local home state legal counsel for the preparation of ancillary documents, if any? Please provide their complete contact information if coordination with their office is necessary.

Mental Disability:

1. If you become mentally disabled during your lifetime, who will serve as your successor Trustee and your agent under a Durable Financial Power of Attorney to make legal and financial decisions for you? You will likely create a Disability Panel that will assist in making a disability determination with the goal of keeping that decision out of the court system. Who do you trust that would know you well enough to participate in a decision to determine your mental capacity? Who should make healthcare decisions for you and be named as your agent under a Durable Healthcare Power of Attorney? This should be a person or persons who are friendly to your Cryonics goals. This will likely be the same person or persons who will be named in your Cryonics Friendly Living Will to contact your standby team at the relevant time to ensure an optimal cryopreservation.
2. If you are unable to communicate your wishes regarding your care for an extended period of time, what are the specific requests/requirements you will want? Do you want to stay in your own home? Do you have long term care insurance that will pay for in-home or alternate care?
3. Do you have a signed contract with a Cryonics organization for your preservation? Attach a copy. Does your Cryonics organization have any specific

suggestions for your care you want to incorporate? Do you wear any special indicia (example, necklace, bracelet) of your intention identifying your interest in cryopreservation?

4. Do you have a separate agreement with an organization that will act in a standby role for the purpose of transporting you at the time of legal death to your chosen Cryonics organization? Do you have any special instructions for them?

5. What are your specific wishes, if any, regarding life-prolonging procedures prior to cryonic suspension?

6. In addition to providing for your care during a period of mental or physical disability, who are the people/pets that you will want your trust assets also to be used for, if any? Do you want to leave any special instructions for them?

If you have pets, will you want to consider their lifetime care and creation of a Pet Trust? Animal Care Trust USA (www.ACT4Pets.org) can assist with the creation of a Pet Trust and provide lifetime care, re-homing and Trustee services.

Legal Death

1. What are the specific things that need to happen at the moment of death? How is this coordinated? Who needs to be put on notice? Please provide any relevant information you want included in your Trust.

2. What happens if you die under circumstances beyond your control and it is impossible for you to have a full-body preservation? Would you want an alternative? If so, what?
3. What contingencies do you want to consider in the event you die under circumstances that are not in a controlled environment? Do you still want your Cryopreservation organization to preserve what they can?
4. If preservation is beyond the realm of possibility? Is it? Then, what are your wishes regarding the final disposition of your body/remains? This could likely include cremation or burial.
5. Do you have loved ones (spouse, children), including pets, that may need to have access to your financial resources after your cryopreservation?

   What kind of instructions do you want to include for them? Lifetime care for health, education and maintenance? Limited Distributions? Outright distributions? There are ways to provide asset protection to protect your assets from the claims of third parties to avoid diminishment of your estate.

   Will your pets be cared for by a Pet Trust?

6. Will any of your loved ones, including pets, be cryopreserved? Are any of them cryopreserved now?

Do you have any cryopreserved embryos or sperm that need to be considered as part of your planning?

7. At your legal death, if your estate is more than the federal estate tax exemption amount, do you want to implement advanced planning that would be designed to eliminate any estate tax consequences? Generally, estate tax minimization strategies will include provisions for charitable organizations. What organizations would you want to benefit?

8. When both you and your loved ones have passed, what are your goals, desires or wishes with respect to the preservation of your assets? Some want to include specific provisions regarding the preservation of specific assets. You are discouraged from being too restrictive or specific because you don't want to put your Trustee in a difficult position.

9. Who will act as successor Trustee for the ongoing management and administration of your assets? To date, we have most successfully worked with Raymond James through advisor, Justin Cairns. For smaller estates that do not meet the large firm estate minimums, we are working with a Florida not for profit firm, Advocates & Guardians for the Elderly & Disabled (AGED - www.TrustAged.org).

Do you have a financial advisor that you will want to have involved for as long as practicable? What about a Certified Public Accountant?

10. Your Trust will include a provision for a Trust Protector. A Trust Protector is someone, not you, not a beneficiary of your Trust and not your Trustee.

    The purpose of the Trust Protector is to provide a resource for amending or revising your Trust based on changed circumstances after your legal death when your trust becomes irrevocable. You may select the identity of your Trust Protector during your lifetime or you may leave the selection up to family, friends, named individuals or even your Trustee (not recommended). You decide which gives you the greatest level of comfort. Many cryonicists are allowing the Teens & Twenties or Biomedical Research and Longevity Society (formerly known as Life Extension Foundation) to either act as Trust Protector or to appoint a Trust Protector for the purpose of communicating with the Trustee during your cryo-preservation.

    The Trust Protector has a very important job. Namely, to provide confirmation on a periodic basis that you are still in active cryopreservation or, ultimately, along with you to advise the Trustee that you have been revived and are once again, entitled to the use of your assets.

    We have gotten a lot of pushback from certain

corporate Trustees regarding their willingness to act proactively with regard to your continued cryopreservation. Some have also indicated an unwillingness to interact with pets and your personal property.

11. If the goal is to maintain your resources until such time as you are reanimated, what period of time are you comfortable with before your Trust might have to be terminated? 90 years? 360 years? In perpetuity? The answer to this question will determine the state in which your trust must be located. Note: Florida has a 360 year Rule Against Perpetuities.

12. Is there any event which you feel would indicate that the purpose for your Personal Revival Trust™ has been frustrated and a termination and distribution of assets is warranted? For example, what if there is a catastrophic disaster while you are in cryopreservation that will unequivocally prevent your reanimation? Then who (persons or organizations) should your assets be distributed to?

13. What incentives, if any, do you want to implement to encourage your Cryonics organization to reanimate you in a timely manner? Do you want to put any restrictions on when the attempt should be made, ie. Only after "x" number of successful reanimations or do you want to be one of the first?

Do you want to include any financial incentives? A percentage of the Trust assets as a bonus is one example.
14. There has recently been some discussion around the possibility of more than one "you" making a claim on your future assets. This could include the reanimated "you", the cloned "you", or a digital "you". Are there others you can think of? Which one would be the acceptable "you" and how should we provide proof positive?

Appendix E
Table of Consanguinity

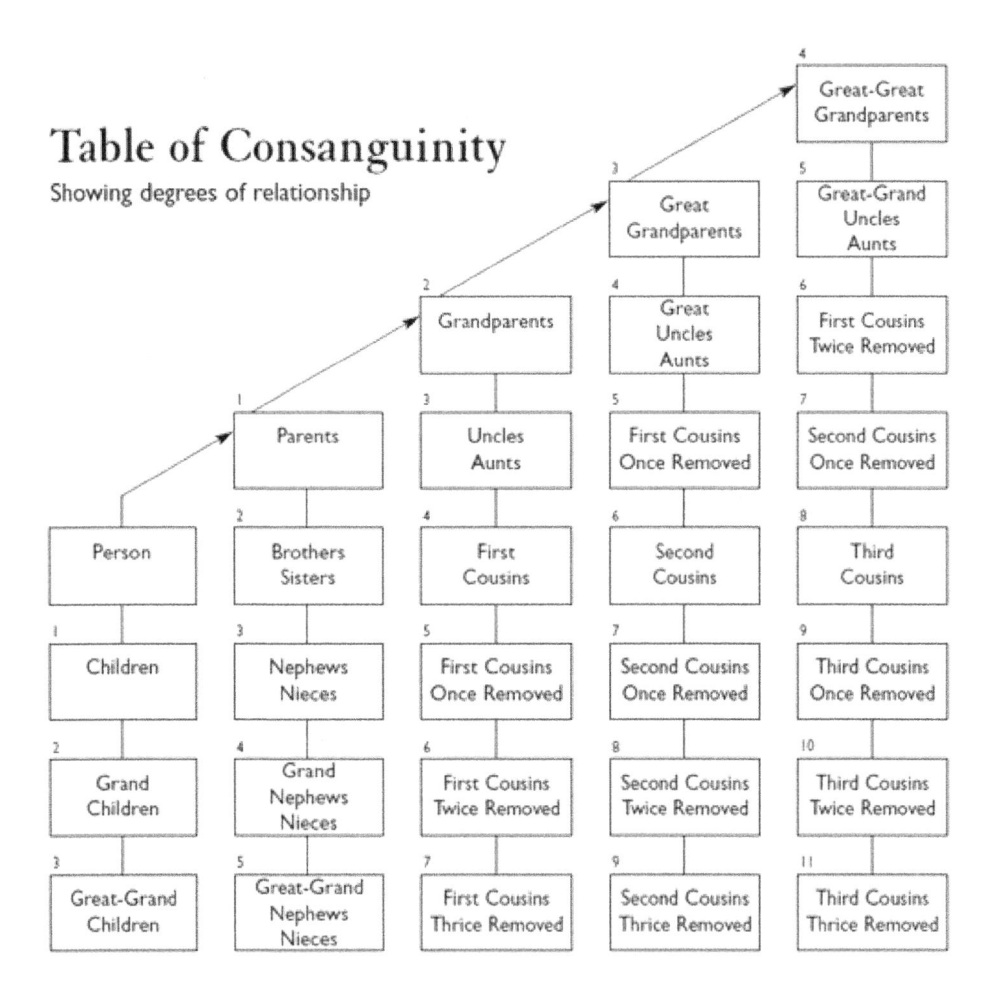

Table of Consanguinity
Showing degrees of relationship

					4 Great-Great Grandparents
				3 Great Grandparents	5 Great-Grand Uncles Aunts
			2 Grandparents	4 Great Uncles Aunts	6 First Cousins Twice Removed
		1 Parents	3 Uncles Aunts	5 First Cousins Once Removed	7 Second Cousins Once Removed
	Person	2 Brothers Sisters	4 First Cousins	6 Second Cousins	8 Third Cousins
	1 Children	3 Nephews Nieces	5 First Cousins Once Removed	7 Second Cousins Once Removed	9 Third Cousins Once Removed
	2 Grand Children	4 Grand Nephews Nieces	6 First Cousins Twice Removed	8 Second Cousins Twice Removed	10 Third Cousins Twice Removed
	3 Great-Grand Children	5 Great-Grand Nephews Nieces	7 First Cousins Thrice Removed	9 Second Cousins Thrice Removed	11 Third Cousins Thrice Removed

Appendix F
7th Annual Dynasty Trust State Rankings Chart

7th Annual Dynasty Trust State Rankings Chart

Rank	State	Perpetuities Statute	Rule Against Perpetuities (40% weight)	State Income Tax (2.5% weight)	Third-Party Spendthrift Trust Provision Effective Against Divorcing Spouse/Child Support (Divorcing Spouse - 7.5% weight/Child Support - 2.5% weight)	Discretionary Trust Protected from Divorcing Spouse/Child Support (2.5% weight)	Domestic Asset Protection Trust State Ranking (10% weight)	Trust Decanting State Ranking (10% weight)	Non-Judicial Settlement Agreement Statute (2.5% weight)	Total Score
1	SD	SD Codified L § 43-5-8	Perpetual	No	Protected	Protected	Ranked #2	Ranked #1	Yes	99.5
2	NV	NV Rev Stat § 111.1031	365 years	No	Protected	Protected	Ranked #1	Ranked #2	Yes	98.5
3	TN	TN Code § 66-1-202(f)	360 years	No (except dividends/ interest on residents)	Protected	Protected	Ranked #4 (tie)	Ranked #3	Yes	95.5
4	AK	AK Stat § 34.27.051	Perpetual / 1,000 years if exercise power of appointment	No	Protected	Protected	Ranked #7	Ranked #7 (tie)	No	94
5	WY	WY Stat § 34-1-139	1,000 years	No	Divorcing spouse = Protected Child support = Not Protected (WY Stat § 4-10-503(b))	Protected	Ranked #10	Ranked #10 (tie)	Yes	89.5
6	RI	RI Gen L § 34-11-38	Perpetual	No (except residents)	Protected	Protected	Ranked #8	Ranked #20	No	87.5
7	OH	Ohio Rev Code § 2131.09(B) and (C)	Perpetual / 1,000 years if exercise power of appointment	No (except residents)	Divorcing spouse = Not Protected Child support = Not Protected (Ohio Rev Code § 5805.02(B)(1))	Protected	Ranked #3	Ranked #6	Yes	86
8	DE	25 DE Code § 503	Perpetual for personal property / 110 years for real estate	No (except residents)	Divorcing spouse = Not Protected Child support = Not Protected (Garretson v. Garretson (1973))	Protected	Ranked #6	Ranked #5	Yes	85
9	IL	765 ILCS 305/1	Perpetual	No (except residents)	Divorcing spouse = Protected Child support = Not Protected (1755 ILCS 5/2-1403 codifying In re Mort (1985))	Protected	None	Ranked #7 (tie)	Yes	84.5
10 (tie)	MO	MO Rev Stat § 456.025	Perpetual	No (except residents)	Divorcing spouse = Not Protected Child support = Not Protected (Mo. Rev. Stat. § 456.5-503(2))	Protected	Ranked #4 (tie)	Ranked #10 (tie)	Yes	84
10 (tie)	NH	NH Rev Stat § 564:24	Perpetual	No (except dividends, interest on residents)	Divorcing spouse = Not Protected Child support = Not Protected (NH Rev Stat § 564-B:5-503(a)(1)-(2))	Protected	Ranked #9	Ranked #4	Yes	84
12	FL	FL Stat § 689.225(2)(f)	360 years	No	Divorcing spouse = Not Protected Child support = Not Protected (FL Stat § 736.0504(2)(a) codifying Bacardi v. White (1985))	Writ of garnishment allowed for spouse, former spouse, child support (FL Stat §736.0503(3); Berlinger v. Casselberry (2013))	None	Ranked #26	Yes	68

"The Domestic Asset Protection Trust State Ranking column is based on the 9th Annual Domestic Asset Protection Trust State Rankings Chart created in April 2018 at http://www.oshins.com/images/DAPT_Rankings.pdf.
"The Trust Decanting State Ranking column is based on the 5th Annual Trust Decanting State Rankings Chart created in January 2018 at http://www.oshins.com/images/Decanting_Rankings.pdf
"This Dynasty Trust State Rankings Chart created in October 2018. Original Dynasty Trust State Rankings Chart created in October 2012.
Copyright © 2012-2018 by Steve Oshins (soshins@oshins.com / www.oshins.com / (702) 341-6000, ext. 2). All rights reserved.

Steve Oshins is a member of the Law Offices of Oshins & Associates, LLC in Las Vegas, Nevada. He was inducted into the NAEPC Estate Planning Hall of Fame® in 2011. He was named one of the 24 "Elite Estate Planning Attorneys" and the "Top Estate Planning Attorney of 2018" by *The Wealth Advisor* and one of the Top 100 Attorneys in *Worth*. He is listed in *The Best Lawyers in America*® which also named him Las Vegas Trusts and Estates/Tax Law Lawyer of the Year in 2012, 2015, 2016 and 2018. He can be reached at 702-341-6000, ext. 2 or soshins@oshins.com. His law firm's website is www.oshins.com.

Contacts and References

Contacts:

Rudi Hoffman, CFP ®, CLU ®, ChFC ®.
(Licensed and Authorized in 49 states and D.C.)
RudiHoffman.com
Rudi@RudiHoffman.com
386-235-7834

Peggy Hoyt, J.D., M.B.A., B.C.S.
(Florida Bar Board Certified Specialist in Wills Trusts and Estates and Elder Law)
The Law Offices of Hoyt and Bryan
HoytBryan.com
Peggy@HoytBryan.com
407-977-8080

Alcor
Alcor.org
7895 E. Acoma Dr. #110
Scottsdale, AZ 85260
877-462-5267

American Cryonics Society
Americancryonics.org
510 S. Mathilda Ave. (Mezzetta Bldg), Suite 8
Sunnyvale, CA 94086

postal mail at: American Cryonics Society
P.O. Box 1509
Cupertino, CA 95015
408-530-9001 or 1-800-523-2001.

Cryonics Institute
Cryonics.org
24355 Sorrentino Ct.
Clinton Township, MI 48035
586-791-5961

References:
(Yes, you should read this section; it's fun!)

Rudi writing: There are a tremendous number of great books available on transhumanism, philosophy, science, technology, agnosticism, and general self-improvement. I have about 900 books on these topics running around in my brain that occasionally work as intended. Personal note: audio / audible books have dramatically improved and changed my life. Here are a few of my favorites.

De Grey, Aubrey. *Ending Aging: The Rejuvenation Breakthroughs That Could End Human Aging in Our Lifetime*. New York: St. Martins Press. 2007. Aubrey is a personal friend—and hero to me and most anyone else following anti-aging and age reversal science. With his trademark

Methuselah beard, Aubrey has become the recognized leader in the charge to end the tsunami of involuntary death. He has created SENS (Strategies for Engineered Negligible Senescence) as an umbrella organization for this purpose. Aubrey is also an "out of the closet" cryonicist. SENS is worth checking out and contributing to, at www.sens.org.

De Wolf, Aschwin and Stephen Bridge. *Preserving Minds, Saving Lives: The Best Cryonics Writings from the Alcor Life Extension Foundation.* Fort Lauderdale, FL: Commercial Printers, Inc. 2015. Anthology of great writing by the history-making thought leaders of Alcor, curated by my good friends Aschwin and Stephen, who remain Cryonics activists.

Diamandis, Peter. *Abundance: Why the Future Is Better Than You Think.* New York: Free Press. 2012. Amazing book by a larger-than-life guy who has started 15 successful companies. Along with Ray Kurzweil, a predictor of the future largely because they are helping to create it.

Diamandis, Peter. *Bold: How to Go Big, Create Wealth, and Impact the World*. New York: Free Press. 2015.

Drexler, K. Eric. *Engines of Creation: The Coming Era of Nanotechnology.* New York: Anchor Books, 1986. One of the first books on nanotech and the amazing possibilities and disruptions possible through Molecular Nanotech. A classic, and responsible for many Cryonics signups. I still remember the thrill I felt reading this book.

Drexler, K. Eric. *Radical Abundance: How a Revolution in Nanotechnology WIll Change Civilization*. New York: Public Affairs. 2013. 27 years after Engines, Drexler hits it out of the park again with the possibilities, as well as the dangers, of molecular manufacturing and medicine.

Ettinger, Robert. *The Prospect of Immortality*. New York: Doubleday. 1964. Kind of THE book that started Cryonics. I treasure my personalized copy. Ettinger was a college professor by trade, but his real contributions are his seminal work about Cryonics and the future. Unflaggingly optimistic, a bit naive about the financial piece of Cryonics, Ettinger remains a hero to many of us involved in Cryonics.

Friedman, Thomas L. *Thank You for Being Late: An Optimist's Guide to Thriving in the Age of Accelerations*. New York: Macmillan Publishing Group. 2016. Well researched and fun to read, documents how fast things are changing, especially since 2007, according to Friedman, the year that a number of curves went pretty much straight up. No wonder we feel we can't keep up! We can't, but not to worry, it will all be for the best.

Halperin, James. *The First Immortal.* New York: Ballantine Books. 1998. One of the best hard-edged (reality based, as opposed to fantasy based) science fiction books about Cryonics. Halperin is an "out of the closet" cryonicist.

Halperin, James. *The Truth Machine.* New York: Ballantine Books. 1996. Hard-edged science fiction with the brilliant premise of a universally accurate, eventually wrist-watch size and completely democratized deception detector and how this changes humans and society.

Hoffman, Rudi. *The Affordable Immortal.* San Bernardino, CA Amazon. 2018. Simply the best book ever written. :) Or, more accurately, the best book ever written about the mechanics and funding of the cryonics signup process.

Hoyt, Peggy R. *All My Children Wear Fur Coats - How to Leave a Legacy for Your Pet*. Legacy Planning Partners. 2020, third edition. Available on Amazon, BarkYours and at Animal Care Trust USA, Inc.(www.ACT4Pets.org). For other books by Peggy Hoyt, visit HoytBryan.com.

Istvan, Zoltan. *The Transhumanist Wager.* Futurity Imagine Media. 2013. A powerful, watershed book. I have curious and contradictory thoughts about this book; it is both one of the best and one of the worst books I have ever read. Make up your own mind, but this one will make you question some paradigms.

Kahneman, Daniel. *Thinking, Fast and Slow*. New York: Farner, Straus, and Giroux. 2011. Brilliant book about cognitive biases and the various experiments used to identify these. I listened to the audiobook twice and wanted to see his charts, so I bought the hard copy.

Kurzweil, Ray. *The Singularity Is Near: When Humans Transcend Biology*. New York: Penguin. 2005. Any of Kurzweil's books, *The Age of Intelligent Machines; The Age of Spiritual Machines: When Computers Exceed Human Intelligence;* or *Fantastic Voyage: Live Long Enough to Life Forever* will blow your mind in a very positive and potentially life changing way. I have been following Ray's career and reading his books since the 1990's. He is the Thomas Edison of our age and the track record on his predictions is remarkably accurate.

McNight, David. *The Power of Zero.* New York: Penguin Random House. 2013. "There's a massive freight train bearing down on the average American investor, and it's coming in the form of higher taxes," … from the forward. Spoiler alert, US income taxes brackets are relatively low, there are compelling macroeconomic reasons indicating taxes for middle class Americans will be dramatically and impactfully higher. Another spoiler alert… 85% of Fortune 500 CEOs have a "Life Insurance Retirement Plan," due to the tax-free withdrawal availability of permanent life insurance. If you have an Index Universal Life policy, you already own a LIRP…

and there are ways to cleverly tweak your policy to increase your tax-free retirement income.

McNight, David. *The Volatility Shield.* New York: Penguin Random House. 2019. A skinny little 30 minute read that could change your retirement strategy. After over 40 years as a highly credentialed financial advisor and Certified Financial Planner, the ideas in this "Financial Novella" caused me to literally re-direct tens of thousands of dollars in my own retirement program. Spoiler alert: Concepts include future income tax considerations and sequence of return risk, spun into an easy to read compelling story format.

Pinker, Steven. *The Better Angels of Our Nature: Why Violence Has Declined*. New York: Viking. 2011. Pretty much what you'd think from the title. Because he understands how much pushback he'll get to this idea, his documentation is exhaustive and meticulous. Pinker's use of the language is about as precise as a human can be.

Pinker, Steven. *Enlightenment Now: The Case for Reason, Science, Humanism, and Progress.* New York: Penguin Random House. 2018. On the cover is a Bill Gates quote about this book, "My new favorite book of all time." I agree. Almost certainly one of the most important and compelling books ever written, with ample evidence to show the overarching arc of human progress measured by multiple metrics. Evidently a lot of people missed the memo about Humanism and the Enlightenment and want to take us back to the bad old days of the Dark Ages, so Pinker has to explain that science is good and superstition is bad.

Ridley, Matt. *The Rational Optimist: How Prosperity Evolves.* New York: Harper Collins. 2010. A truly wonderful book and audiobook. Ridley is a geneticist by training, but this book is about human progress. Has there ever been a better chapter title than the first in this book, "When Ideas Have Sex"?

Glossary of Terms

Alcor - The Alcor Life Extension Foundation, a California not-for-profit corporation, located at 7895 East Acoma Drive, Suite 100, Scottsdale, Arizona 85260. https://www.alcor.org/.

American Cryonics Society - A member-run Cryonics organization headquartered in Sunnyvale, CA, founded in 1969. https://www.americancryonics.org/.

Biostasis - Complete arrest of biological activity. Cryonic suspension is one form of biostasis. Also known as cryostasis.

Clinical Death - Death as judged by the medical observation of cessation of vital functions. It is typically identified with the cessation of heartbeat and respiration, though modern resuscitation methods and life-support systems have required the introduction of the alternative concept of brain death. (Oxford English Dictionary)

Cryogenics - Not to be confused with Cryonics (see below). In physics, cryogenics is the production and behaviour of materials at very low temperatures. A person who studies elements that have been subjected to extremely cold temperatures is called a cryogenicist.

Cryonics (not Cryogenics) - The cryopreservation of humans with intent of future resuscitation. Laws currently require Cryonics to be performed after legal death, but death is not part of the basic idea of Cryonics. The purpose of Cryonics is to preserve life.

Cryonics Institute - The Cryonics Institute is a non-profit membership organization made up of people seeking to pursue Cryonics' "Prospect of Immortality" for themselves and their families. They are located at 24355 Sorrentino Court, Clinton Township, MI 48035.

Cryonics Organization - an organization like Alcor or The Cryonics Institute whose purpose is to provide education and cryopreservation to persons interested in cryonic preservation.

Cryonic Suspension - The experimental practice of maintaining patients currently classified as legally "dead" at extremely low temperatures for possible treatment by future medicine. Also known as cryopreservation.

Cryonicist - An individual who has actually completed the legal paperwork and funding arrangements with a legitimate Cryonics organization.

Cryopreservation (Cryopreserved) - Preservation of cells or tissue at cryogenic (below -80 degC) temperatures for an indefinite period of time.

Cryostasis - Another word for cryopreservation.

Death (also see Legal Death) - A government's official recognition that a person has died, generally through the issuance of a death certificate. Typically, an individual would be considered dead or to have experienced legal death upon sustaining either a cessation of circulatory and respiratory function or the cessation of all functions of the entire brain, including the brain stem.

Dewar - A cryogenic storage dewar (named after James Dewar) is a specialized type of vacuum flask used for storing cryogens (such as liquid nitrogen or liquid helium), whose boiling points are much lower than room temperature.

Future - What is yet to come.

Hypoxia - A serious complication that continues to be a leading cause of morbidity and mortality.

Ischemia - Inadequate or absent blood circulation. Ischemic injury is caused by diminished or absent blood flow. The main mechanism of injury in ischemia is hypoxia (see above).

Legal Death - The recognition under the law of a particular jurisdiction that a person is no longer alive based on current technology and medical understanding. The point at which a medical professional has pronounced "death."

Nanotechnology - Technology with components measured in billionths of a meter.

Patient - An individual in cryonic suspension or other form of biostasis who is under the care and custody of a Cryonics organization.

Patient Care - The ongoing activities required to maintain Patients in cryonic suspension or other forms of biostasis.

Personal Revival Trust™ - A proprietary, customized trust designed to preserve the assets of a cryonicist while in biostasis to increase the likelihood assets will be available at the time of reanimation.

Revival, Resuscitation or Reanimation - The anticipated future processes of restoring or repairing Patients to a condition that will allow them to be considered legally alive, functional, and independent.

Rule Against Perpetuities - Laws limiting the amount of time a trust can be maintained legally.

Standby - Preparations and onsite waiting for legal death prior to cryopreservation.

Suspended Animation - A temporary cessation of most vital functions without death. Cryonics will not be considered suspended animation until it is reversible in practice, not just theory.

Suspension Funding - The money or other assets donated or paid to a Cryonics organization at the time a "suspension member" enters biostasis and becomes a "Patient." A portion of this funding may be reserved for Patient Care expenses.

Suspension Member - An individual who has made the legal and financial arrangements with a Cryonics organization for cryonic suspension or other form of biostasis, but who has not yet entered biostasis and become a Patient.

Vitrification - An ice-free process in which over 60% of the water inside cells is replaced with protective chemicals. It permits the solidification of a solution without the formation of ice crystals.

About the Author, Peggy Hoyt

Peggy R. Hoyt, J.D., M.B.A., B.C.S.
(Florida Bar Board Certified Specialist in Wills, Trusts and Estates and Elder Law)

Background: Peggy is a Stetson University graduate receiving her B.B.A., cum laude, in 1981, her M.B.A. in 1982 and her J.D., cum laude, in 1993. Her work experience includes time as a college recruiter, financial consultant, account executive and chief financial officer before entering law school. She is a founding partner of Hoyt & Bryan, LLC. Peggy is one of a handful of attorneys in Florida who is dual certified by the Florida Bar in Wills, Trusts, and Estates and in Elder Law.

Peggy is the founder and CEO of Animal Care Trust USA, Inc., a 501c(3) not for profit organization, whose two-fold mission is to educate pet parents of the world how to keep Loved Pets in Loving Homes through the use of Pet Trusts and to provide lifetime care solutions and Pet Trustee services. She hosts a weekly "Pawcast" entitled "All My Children Wear Fur Coats" where she interviews animal experts in all facets of pet care and wellness, rescue, and ensuring our pets have forever homes.

Experience: Peggy practices in the areas of family wealth and legacy counselling, including trust and estate planning and administration, elder law, small business creation, succession and exit planning, real estate transactions and animal law. In addition to her law degree, she holds a Florida real estate license. Peggy formerly held a NASD Series 7 license and health, life and variable annuities licenses. She serves as a certified FINRA Arbitrator and is a Florida Mediator concentrating in family business, estate administration, and animal law issues. Peggy is a former adjunct professor of Animal Law with Barry University College of Law.

Author/Public Speaker: Peggy is the author of *All My Children Wear Fur Coats – How to Leave a Legacy to Your Pet*, an informative and inspirational guide for pet owners who want to include their pets as part of their estate plans.

She is a co-author of the following books with Candace M. Pollock: *Special People, Special Planning – Creating a Safe Legal Haven for Families with Special Needs,* designed to educate families about the planning options and protections for their special needs family members; *Loving Without a License – An Estate Planning Survival Guide for Unmarried Couples and Same*

Sex Partners, created to address the unique planning needs of unmarried individuals in today's society; *A Matter of Trust – The Importance of Personal Instructions,* stressing the importance of supplementing legal estate planning with personal instructions; *Women in Transition – Navigating the Legal and Financial Challenges in Your Life,* created for all women as they learn, live and grow throughout their lives. Peggy is co-author with Scott Farnsworth of *Like a Library Burning – Sharing and Saving a Lifetime of Stories,* which addresses protecting and passing on a lifetime of stories.

Peggy is co-author with Deborah Roser of *Thank Everybody for Everything! Grow your Life and Your Business with Gratitude*, and the companion five-year gratitude journal, *Gratitude Expressions, Straight Talk! About Estate Planning and Straight Talk! What to Do When Someone Dies*. Her most recent books are *What's the Deal With...Estate Planning* and *What's the Deal With...Estate Administration.*

This is her first book with Rudi Hoffman.

Peggy speaks at the local, regional and national levels on estate planning and elder law topics including pet planning, special needs planning, and planning for unmarried couples and same sex partners. She is also highly regarded for her workshops on gratitude marketing and law office management. She has been featured on CNN Financial News, the Wall Street Journal and the Orlando Sentinel for her dedication to pet planning.

Education:
Stetson University, B.B.A (Marketing/Management 1981), *cum laude*
Stetson University, M.B.A. (Finance 1982)
Stetson University College of Law, J.D. (1993), cum laude, Phi Delta Phi

Professional and Civic Affiliations:
WealthCounsel and ElderCounsel, Member
Central Florida Estate Planning Council, Member, Past President, Member
The Florida Bar, member; Past Chair for the Solo and Small Firm Section and past chair of the Animal Law Section.

Peggy can be easily reached at:
Email: Peggy@HoytBryan.com
Phone: 407-977-8080

About the Author, Rudi Hoffman

Rudi Hoffman, CFP®, CLU®, ChFC®

Rudi Hoffman, author of "The Affordable Immortal: Maybe You CAN Beat Death and Taxes" (Amazon, 2018), is a fellow human being, sharing about 99.9% of the same DNA you have. He works hard at being a genuinely good human and has a passion for sharing ideas that matter with his fellow travelers on the planet.

He lives in the beautiful village of Port Orange, Florida, with his wife Dawn, administrator for Rudi Hoffman CFP®, and with their two spoiled dogs.

Professionally, he holds the top three credentials in financial planning, CFP®, CLU®, and ChFC®. Licensed since 1978, he maintains life insurance and securities licenses in 49 states and in the District of Columbia.

He is in the top 1% of life insurance brokers worldwide, enabling hundreds of millions of dollars in life insurance benefits to be available to wonderful and grateful clients.

Rudi is a popular speaker at national and international cryonics and anti-aging conferences, as well as for local and civic groups. Along with Neal VanDeRee, he co-chaired and founded the First Cryonics Symposium International in 2018. He has been the subject of numerous television and podcast interviews.

Rudi is the world's leading authority on funding and financial matters relating to cryopreservation. He is overly proud that more than 70% of the funded cryonicists on Earth have been assisted in their cryopreservation financing by his firm. He is also humbled by the responsibility this represents. He would be pleased and honored to have you view some website videos, fill out a website form, and schedule an appointment to talk with him.

Rudi can be easily reached at:
Email: Rudi@RudiHoffman.com
Phone: 386-235-7834
Website with "Quote Request" form and short videos under the "Cryonics" tab: www.RudiHoffman.com

Made in the USA
Las Vegas, NV
30 March 2021